David Rowley was born the same week the Beatles second album was released. He attended Central Foundation Boys School, London and Keele University. He began writing his first Beatles' book in 1991 which became *Beatles For Sale*, 2002 and was followed by *Help! 50 songwriting, recording and career tips used by the Beatles,* 2008. He lives in London and works as a journalist.

ALL TOGETHER NOW

The abc of the Beatles songs and albums

David Rowley

Front cover illustration: Howard McWilliam
Sub-editing: Christine Rowley

Extracts from Paul McCartney: Many Years From Now by Barry Miles,
published by Secker & Warburg. Reprinted by permission of
The Random House Group Limited

Matador
9 Priory Business Park,
Wistow Road, Kibworth Beauchamp,
Leicestershire. LE8 0RX
Tel: (+44) 116 279 2299
Fax: (+44) 116 279 2277
Email: books@troubador.co.uk
Web: www.troubador.co.uk/matador

ISBN 978 178088 440 0

British Library Cataloguing in Publication Data.
A catalogue record for this book is available from the British Library.

Typeset by Troubador Publishing Ltd, Leicester, UK

Matador is an imprint of Troubador Publishing Ltd

Printed and bound in the UK by TJ International, Padstow, Cornwall

For Simon Wenman and Simon Glass whom I first played guitar with.

INTRODUCTION

The Beatles stand up to scrutiny. The longer and closer one listens, the more complex and talented they emerge. Attempts to find an Achilles heel, to find them failing in some aspect, are either fruitless or negligible.

Whilst others have equalled them sporadically, none has the same duration or rate of output. Analysis of why this is so is neglected. Yet for anyone who has been entranced by popular music, and who has learnt guitar, written songs, formed a group, played live, recorded, however modestly, this should be a fascination. What is their formula?

The best explanation lies in the period between August 1960 and December 1962, when they were probably the hardest-working musicians in the world. On their first trip to Hamburg, aged 17-19, they played sometimes eight hours a night so hungry were they to become professional musicians – a feat only the young and naive would attempt. The hours were driven by demand. The city had a tolerant attitude to prostitution and strip shows which made it a magnet for sailors and thrill-seekers alike, which in turn created demand for a surfeit of bars and nightclubs and an appreciation for frenzied rock 'n' roll. In this rarefied environment, they were given accommodation and just enough money for food, clothing and guitar strings, in return for playing cover versions of US hits six days a week, an opportunity that has been rarely seen since. One might liken it to a rock 'n' roll stage school.

In Hamburg they regularly played to people who

knew little of them, while in Liverpool and its surrounds, there were also many one-night stands. To survive they learnt how to win over unfamiliar audiences and how to stay one small step ahead of expectations.

Uppermost in their skills was the use of vocals. With all the group contributing backing vocals, this added a layer of sound similar to the chords played on an electric organ – giving a more versatile sound than the average guitar group, while John and Paul's mix of octaves brought an operatic sense of story-telling and contrast.

They learnt the art of songwriting through playing between 300-500 cover versions live. This provided a host of ideas, tricks and lessons from which to draw. Some of this was subconscious, so numerous were their hours clocked up on stage, some of it not so. George Harrison once claimed that if you named him any Beatles' song, he could tell the record upon which it was based. John, who stole records, a guitar, an amplifier and a harmonica during these hungry days pre-fame, certainly lost no sleep over re-working someone else's tune. He once mischievously explained that he would take another's song and change it to the point where he could not be sued. However, George's claim served as a dig at his band-mates, whose status soared while he worked with less ego and ambition. Paul, for example, claimed no knowledge of the origin of 'Yesterday' and John, likewise, for 'Across the Universe'. Indeed, the songs they covered – much of them 1950s rock 'n' roll – only partly explain their craft. These typically use three or four chords, unlike the five, six or seven of a Lennon/McCartney composition. The odd chord change (Del Shannon's 'Runaway') or an arrangement (Maurice Williams and the Zodiacs' 'Stay'), was copied, but there was always some thrilling, inexplicable alchemy added.

Lyrically, too, there is a disconnect between these songs and their own work. The 300 cover versions documented by Mark Lewisohn in *The Beatles Recording Sessions*, are peppered with clichéd gambits about heartbreak, true love and dances. When Lennon/McCartney replicated this, it tended to come with a twist. The cheeky smut hidden amid the endearments on their first big hit, 'Please Please Me', mocks any traditions it borrows from. The rhymes of 'She Loves You' and 'Can't Buy Me Love' are over-familiar, but the way they are directed at a third party in a celebratory tone, as if a community message, shifts the love song from personal to universal. This follows no obvious precedent, certainly none found in rock 'n' roll. While naturally bold they were also a product of the 1960s, a period prosperous, confident and open to change after years of austerity. The utopian visions, the cheeky phrases and references to mind-expanding drugs would not have been publicly acceptable a decade before.

The list of attributes derived from playing nightly is lengthy and an expectation as a covers band to keep up with the latest hits and to follow their audiences' tastes is another factor in their success. It goes some way to explaining their constant evolution and ability to stay up to date, whether it was the Latin rhythm on 'P.S. I Love You' or the heavy metal of 'I Want You (She's so Heavy)'. Such demands too gave them a work ethic that helped them respond to their onerous contract for an album every six months. One of their best, *Rubber Soul*, was written and recorded in the space of two months. John, in his solo career, took the process to its ultimate extent with 'Instant Karma', a song written and recorded in one day.

Intense and prolonged training explains much of what made the Beatles great – but not everything. In his book *The Outliers*, Malcolm Gladwell uses the Beatles as an example of what he has termed the 10,000 hour rule, which states practising for this long will lead to success.

However, the rule is probably best applied to fellow Liverpudlian bands, The Searchers and Gerry and the Pacemakers, for whom training overcame limited ability. Long hours can produce success, but it is not the only explanation for what made the Beatles special.

John was an extraordinarily coherent communicator and the directness of his lyrics has few precedents. His articulate summary of his deepest thoughts is seductive and precious unlike the disposable sentiments of most pop. A troubled childhood was one trigger in his need to connect with others and find love, whilst his dyslexia appeared to go hand in hand with compensatory intellectual skills as recent research of the condition suggests.

Paul benefited from his relationship with his father who, as an accomplished pianist, provided an early musical education. Both felt a need to make up for the tragedy of losing their mothers as teenagers, both came from a city with strong communal traditions, a city known for open, witty, and blunt conversation. Crucially, both were driven by a fear of being surpassed by the other. When John wrote 'Help!', Paul wrote 'Yesterday'. When Paul wrote 'Michelle', John wrote 'Girl'. When John wrote 'Strawberry Fields Forever', Paul wrote 'Penny Lane'. When John wrote 'Julia', Paul wrote 'Let It Be'. Songwriting took place in a spirit of competition, unlike the inefficient dictatorships of groups with one key songwriter.

Their multi-faceted career progression is much overlooked in understanding what made them tick. They were first a skiffle band, a covers band with vast experience of playing to domestic and foreign audiences, then a boy band, and finally a hybrid of rock/ pop, with at the end of their career some of the sensibilities of alternative/ indie pop groups. The popularity of dividing their career into two halves labelled 'early' and 'mature' has encouraged artists to ignore the first stages and concentrate on the last two. Focusing on the latter has become an aspiration for those who need little encouragement to write about their deepest thoughts. Arguably such artists never confront how to connect with their audiences. Certainly from *Rubber Soul* to *Abbey Road* the group explored the limits of what could be achieved within a pop song, but it would be wrong to assume their earlier years were naïve and lacking in significant depth. Their initial targets had been to write teen girl-orientated songs, which would earn them money and make them famous. That they succeeded spectacularly where others had failed in this aim does not suggest immaturity at all. Given John's art school background and love of surreal writers such as Lewis Carroll and Edward Lear, there is no reason why he should not have tapped such influences earlier if the financial incentive had been there.

The cleverness of their earliest compositions is apparent, even with the much-overlooked 'There's a Place' from *Please Please Me*. Where one might expect its key moment to arrive in the chorus or the hook or a repeated harmony, it is instead at a single line in a verse. At 0.47 the singing reaches a crescendo, with John addressing the listener with extra emphasis. He is backed throughout by Paul, but here for the only time George joins. The effect is electric and entirely instinctive. It turns a fairly rough, unsteady performance into something magical and worth listening to 50 years later.

Analysing the songs

There have been several notable analyses of the Beatles music. Steve Turner's *Hard Day's Write* focuses on the incidents behind the lyrics, featuring the thrilling discovery of Melanie Cohen, the real life person Paul depicted in 'She's Leaving Home'. Jonathan Gould's *Can't Buy Me Love* interweaves sociological themes with analyses of key songs and remarkably decodes the lyrics to 'I am the Walrus' for references from Lewis Carroll's *Through the Looking Glass*.

Ian McDonald's *Revolution in the Head* exposes where the music echoes the lyrics' emotions, drawing fascinating observations around late period tracks such as 'Penny Lane', 'I am The Walrus', 'Revolution 9', 'Eleanor Rigby' and in particular 'Tomorrow Never Knows'. Indeed, his high praise for *Revolver* has elevated it to being considered the Beatles' best. But there is a reliance on musical terms not found in the Beatles' vernacular and where he cannot find complexity, as on earlier work or tracks such as 'Here Comes the Sun' and 'Let It Be' his instinct is to belittle. Also, he uses the Beatles' achievements as a cudgel to attack the failings of modern music, which is an easy, but ultimately mean approach. This is the polar opposite of my intentions and I wrote, *Help! 50 songwriting, recording and career tips used by the Beatles* (2008), partly to redress this.

My first analysis, *Beatles for Sale* (2002), in hindsight is naive. The result of 11 years part-time research, it allowed in too much of my own tastes. It also readily used accepted popular beliefs. As Philip Norman noted in the updated Beatles' biography *Shout!*, their story has become like some ancient myth 'reduced to a string of worn-smooth legends and half-truths by endless fireside telling and retelling'. The odd sentence or two remains from *Beatles For Sale* here, but it has been vigorously re-thought.

Is another analysis needed? The answer surely is, only if there are enough revelations, and this has been my benchmark. A new perspective helps and an alphabetical lay-out is a simple idea that no-one has yet tried in print.

The way this jumbles songs from different eras creates unexpected connections, while a chronological listing often disappoints for showing what little connection each song has to the one recorded a day before.

Scrutiny of the original discs and tracking down the music the Beatles listened to, such as the songs they are known to have performed live has been key research, as has working out the chord progressions and the riffs, though many excellent websites now do an excellent job of this. Generally the internet has made sleuthing easier. YouTube contains rare out-takes and live performances. I made two visits to the now defunct John Lennon museum outside Tokyo in Japan, where handwritten lyrics were on display. Then there are the numerous interviews the Beatles gave. Some tracked down online, some from scanning old newspapers and magazines picked up at Beatles' fairs. These are all of interest, but the best still remain the marathon conversations with John in *Rolling Stone* (1970) and *Playboy* (1980). The views in each have proved so influential that the normally taciturn Paul was forced to reply with *Many Years from Now (1998)*. All three accounts are fruitful after repeated reading and have helped set the tone for *All Together Now*. So if I have been rough on certain songs, e.g. 'Little Child', 'I'm Happy Just to Dance with You' it is partly because John and Paul were, if anything, even more dismissive.

Again in the spirit the Beatles set themselves, I have sought to write in their style, being quick to the point, pacey and bold.

NOTES TO THE TEXT

Credits
For songwriting credits (*Lennon*) or (*McCartney*) indicates that as far as is known John or Paul was the sole writer. (*Lennon/McCartney*) indicates that John was the dominant writer or had the initial idea and vice versa.

Musical terminology
The middle eight in its purest form refers to a section of a song that appears in its middle and is eight bars long. The Beatles used it to add a change of tone, texture or pace and to make the return of the final chorus and verse more dramatic or welcoming for the listener.

Recording dates and takes
Listed with each song are recording details taken from Mark Lewisohn's *The Beatles' Recording Sessions*. Where a number of recording takes are listed for a song, this is largely for songs where all four Beatles are playing the majority of what the listener hears as a live performance. Where take numbers are not included, this is for songs such as 'Michelle' or 'Getting Better' where a simple backing track of drums, rhythm guitar and bass were recorded in a couple of takes and then transformed by numerous overdubs.

Calculations of the hours spent recording and mixing each album are taken from Lewisohn too. These, though, should only be taken as estimates. The hours logged for the later albums are likely to be too high, as by then the group would often turn up late for a session booked in their name. In the early stages of their recording career they were more likely to turn up promptly and make full use of the allotted hours given, such was their tight schedule.

Instruments
The standard Beatles song has John on rhythm guitar, George on lead and/ or rhythm guitar, Paul on bass and Ringo on drums. Paul also takes the majority of the piano/ keyboard parts. Where this line-up differs I have sought to point it out.

ABBEY ROAD

Album released 26th September 1969

The last album recorded by the Beatles and their second biggest-selling after *Sgt Pepper's*.

At 47 minutes and 23 seconds this is the longest Beatles' album.

Recorded between February and August 1969 in 283 hours, mixed in 112 hours

Slick harmonies were achieved as rancour simmered between John, Paul and George. A split was being openly talked of, but as negotiations for a hike in royalties were underway they knuckled down to business. Even so, a united front was lacking and there were few of the all-night sessions which marked their previous work. Instead, basic tracks were completed with overdubs that did not require everyone's presence, particularly John's, often leaving the song's writer alone to insure a satisfactory outcome. Paul later said his erstwhile partner was no longer interested in anything he hadn't written himself and he certainly was peripheral to the recording of George's 'Something' and 'Here Comes The Sun'.

John, in turn, damned the album as over-slick and expressed regret that *Let It Be* had not been their last, as he felt its 'shittiness' would have broken what he described as 'the Beatles' myth'. Paul, conversely, wanted to go out on a high and worked relentlessly with George Martin and chief engineer Geoff Emerick to make the album special. Indeed, the sound definition on *Abbey Road* has made it a favourite with the public if not all of its critics. On tracks like 'She Came in through The Bathroom Window' the vocal, piano, guitar, each individual bass note and drum has its own breathing space. If *Sgt Pepper's* was about achieving fantastical sounds, here it was about high fidelity. Using newly-available 8-track recording machines, their skill for harmonisation is now crystal clear, as is the thrill of hearing all the moving parts of their hardest rock'n'roll, 'Come Together' and 'I Want You (She's so Heavy)' .

ACROSS THE UNIVERSE

Lennon

Four official versions exist, the most for a Beatles' song. These are found on *Let It Be, Past Masters, Anthology 3 and Let It Be Naked*. Each mix is taken from a basic recording completed on 8th February 1968.

Space and airplane flight have often been used in song to allude to drug highs – the 'universe' referred to here is John's mind. Long in thrall to hallucinogenics, he teased a journalist in 1980 who asked whether he still took LSD, by stating "people are still visiting the cosmos". Here an out-of-body experience where people and objects can be seen or heard but to which he is impervious, are described as if floating in space.

John also sought 'the cosmos' through spirituality and in the chorus he refers to Indian guru, the Maharishi, who had taught him transcendental meditation. Indeed, he recognised the dangers of drugs and initially credited the Maharishi as replacing this dependency. His need for salvation is borne out in an unsatisfactory recording, which he blamed on being "psychologically destroyed" by LSD.

While Paul had brought to life John's previous impressionistic songs, here he played a negligible role and it is tempting to believe he did not try his hardest. John's accusation that Paul sabotaged some of his work by introducing "looseness, casualness and experimentation" is most often linked to 'Across the Universe'. But it is also easy to understand Paul's frustration with his partner's

2

light-headedness and the greater creative input he normally gave to John, compared with the more haphazard help he received in return. One wonders, too, if George Martin was having his patience tested.

The problems started with an unusual metre which no one seemed sure how to arrange (the rhythm of the lyrics is set by onomatopoeia – in the first line the words patter out like rain falling onto paper). A sitar and even humming were tried. All failed and instead of becoming the next single, 'Lady Madonna' took its place and the tapes were shelved. During the *Let It Be* project, John attempted a remake, but the four different mixes now in existence are all taken from the original 1968 recording.

ACT NATURALLY

A No.1 Country and Western hit for Buck Owens in June 1963 that was written by Johnny Russell. However, for the act of selling it to Owens, Voni Morrison was given a 50% credit.
Recorded in 13 takes on 17th June 1965
Found on *Help!*

Suffering his usual fate of a rushed recording, Ringo's flat vocal delivers this self-pitying tale without humour. By comparison when Buck Owens sings the original, the audience is invited to laugh with him and his love of satire is evident in the way he and his band would put on mop-top wigs and play 'Twist and Shout' live to acknowledge the Beatles' cover.

Knowing of Ringo's unease at his performance, months later John cruelly introduced it live by saying "Now here's Ringo all nervous and out of tune, to sing something for you". In the same humour Owens originally intended, onstage Ringo later introduced it that way himself.

ALL I'VE GOT TO DO

Lennon
"That's me trying to do Smokey Robinson again". John '80
Recorded in 15 takes on 11th September 1963
Found on *With the Beatles*

Whilst John was the same age as Smokey Robinson, he mastered songwriting much later. For him initially the biggest financial rewards were in playing live in Hamburg and Liverpool. In the USA, a proliferation of independent radio stations and small record labels meant the most exciting opportunities were in recording. In this way, Smokey Robinson made his first record at 18 with the Miracles and had his first national hit, 'Bad Girl', aged 19. By the time of the Beatles' second album he had released 17 singles with the Miracles, and the 13th of these, 'What's So Good About Goodbye', was used as a framework here. Both share a stuttered opening, the first, second and fifth lines sung slowly and the third and fourth sung fast. The fifth line repeats a key phrase from the start too. Play them together and they are nearly interchangeable.

Such early soul music spoke to John for being sung as if genuinely from the heart, a contrast to the rehearsed emotions then used in pop. Notably, his vocal (a rarity for the album, being unaccompanied and single-tracked) displays a rare emotional vulnerability. By contrast, his lyrics are still largely clichéd rhymes, lacking the brutal honesty he showed in interviews from this time. When asked if Dick Rowe, the boss at Decca was kicking himself for turning down the Beatles, John said: "I hope he kicks himself to death."

ALL MY LOVING

McCartney
"The trouble is he wants the fans adulation as well as mine too....He

can't see that my feelings for him are real and the fans' are fantasy."
Jane Asher talking about Paul in January 1964.
Recorded in 14 takes on 30th July 1963
Found on *With the Beatles*

Paul's lyrics are a love letter to fans whose town and cities the Beatles visited on tour and then departed from the next day. He took inspiration after witnessing Roy Orbison compose 'Pretty Woman' on their tour bus, based on an experience he'd had hours before. What must have dawned on Paul was the idea that you could write from immediate experience as well as make-believe.

Unlike most Lennon/McCartney compositions of this era, months were spent perfecting it. The extra effort is evident in the way the soaring vocal melody offsets the descending chords, though the *coup de grace* was its studio performance. Like 'Twist And Shout' before it, 'All My Loving' was saved for the end of a full day's playing, when the band was melding with precision and power, particularly John and George's guitars. The performance, despite its breakneck speed, ends as it starts, with each instrument precisely in time.

In the early days John used his position as nominal leader to assert his way, which might explain why 'All My Loving' was never released as a single.

ALL TOGETHER NOW

McCartney
Paul, John and Ringo sing, but George is absent.
Recorded in nine takes on 12th May 1967
Found on *Yellow Submarine*

In his 24th year Paul McCartney fearlessly tackled with great success a wide array of musical styles from heavy rock, 1930s pop, chamber music, jazz-rock, Motown to psychedelia. To add to this list he wrote a three-chord children's sing-along for the *Yellow Submarine* cartoon with a chorus so catchy for a while it became a chant by fans at football matches. Indeed, so confident was he, that this became the first Beatles' song to be self-produced in George Martin's absence. A pared-down arrangement, its main gimmick is a closely miked acoustic guitar. Otherwise it is notable for lyrics in which Paul, as all-round rock star about town, cannot resist hiding a little smut.

AND I LOVE HER

Words: McCartney/ Lennon Music: McCartney/Harrison
John made a claim for having written the middle eight, which Paul disputed.
"The first ballad I impressed myself with", Paul 98
Paul had the chords and the melody, but George dreamt up the opening four note guitar riff.
Recordings on 25th and 26th February 1964 were scrapped, the finished version was made over lunchtime on 27th February. Over 21 takes in total several arrangements were tried out. At the time no other Beatles' song had been given such time and attention.
Found on *A Hard Day's Night*

Paul arrived as a professional songwriter with this exquisite composition that showcases a number of advanced tricks. Using the word 'and' at the start of the title was his self-conscious effort to be clever as he admitted, but there is little mannered about the way he tells a third person about his bliss and then switches to a personal conversation with his girlfriend, Jane Asher, for the middle eight. More bravado came from moving up a subtle shift from F#m to Gm for the guitar solo. There is the illusion too, that the opening (and closing) riff changes each time it is played, by alternating the chords behind it. The repeated use of the words 'dark' and 'die' are given power by the predominant minor chords, while the reference to stars is echoed in the way George's arpeggio mimics a film music approximation of the sound of twinkling stars. For Paul, teen affairs are over and this is a classy romance to which he is aspiring.

AND YOUR BIRD CAN SING

Lennon/McCartney

A version recorded on 20th April 1966 was scrapped, the finished version was made in 10 takes on 26th April

Found on *Revolver*

Whilst rare today, the rock lyric that bemoans those that value possessions over friendship was common in the 1960s. The Rolling Stones' 'Play With Fire' and '19th Nervous Breakdown' were about spoilt rich girls, as were Bob Dylan's 'Like A Rolling Stone' and 'Queen Jane Approximately'. The Kinks had written fantasies of rich men's demise on 'Most Exclusive Residence for Sale' and 'Sunny Afternoon' and John, to his credit, satirised his own life as a lonely rock star in a mansion on 'Nowhere Man'. He returned to the theme by addressing 'And Your Bird Can Sing' to a person whose 'possessions' stop them from being 'awoken'. Exactly whom he was thinking of is unclear. Some cite Paul, who was busy exploring the London art world seeing many 'wonders'. Or is it Mick Jagger? The lofty status of the Stones' lead singer was enhanced by his beautiful girlfriend and singer, Marianne Faithfull. Another theory says Frank Sinatra had made disparaging remarks about the Beatles in a magazine in which he revealed his common usage of the word 'bird' as slang. Possibly John had several targets including himself, but he did not reveal whom, only referring to the song as a 'horror', showing that whatever the concept, it had failed.

His remarks surely did not refer to the guitar playing.

A dazzling, dynamic solo was achieved by two guitars playing simultaneously but differing for the odd note. The technique had been used on 'Eight Miles High' by the Byrds, which is alluded to in the title – in the same way George's instrumental 'Cry For a Shadow' referred to the Shadows.

ANNA (GO TO HIM)

Arthur Alexander, who wrote 'Anna' in 1962, ended up as a bus driver.
Recorded in three takes on the evening of 11th February 1963
Found on *Please Please Me*

Arthur Alexander's original 'Anna' is sung in the tone of someone who has been pitifully hurt; when he sings 'go to him' he is broken. By contrast, John's rendition covers hurt, strength and defiance. From him the words 'go to him' are an order. The interpretations echo their relative fortunes; whereas in Alexander's reading you fear for his future, John is ultimately in charge of his destiny, he will clearly love again. So where Alexander refers to the girl as 'darling' and sings that she will be free once she gives back the ring he bought her, John curtly omits this word and changes this line to the imperious 'I will set you free'.

The contrast is in the music too. On Alexander's 'Anna' the lush piano and weeping strings heighten the melodrama, while the clipped, clanging guitar notes here emphasise the steel brought to the words. The standout is John's powerful vocal, which realises unseen dramatic potential from the bridge (0.58-1.32).

ANOTHER GIRL

McCartney

Described by Paul as merely a 'filler' track to make up an album.
Recorded on 15th February 1965 with a guitar overdub the following day.
Found on *Help!*

Mid-February 1965, Paul lay in a sunken bath at a grand villa in Tunisia, while his colleagues and friends shivered back at home. Finding the large marble room conducive to singing and contemplating his general good fortune, he concocted a self-satisfied tale of revenge on any woman who might have not treated him in the regal style he was starting to enjoy.

On return to London a week later, this sense of grandeur lingered. In the recording studio he lost patience with George's attempts at a guitar solo and played it himself, as if to act out his proclamation that he 'don't take' what he does not want. The solo is certainly spirited, but lopsided too, but no-one was going to tell him otherwise. The lead vocal and guitar drown out a murky backing, suggesting the Beatles were in no mood to perfect the track – possibly friction between George and Paul lessened co-operation.

ANTHOLOGY
Released as *Anthology 1, 2 and 3,* 1995-96

At its best, this three album collection of out-takes and first-drafts tells us how the Beatles learnt to use the studio as a laboratory. A prime example being the early run-through of 'And I Love Her'; possibly the first song they completely rethought in the studio. It evolved over three days from the commonplace to the extraordinary, a miniature slice of classical pop that expanded their world. Its success hooked them into the idea of the studio, or at least Abbey Road studios, as a place where song-writing could be continued. There were many successes but also a few dead-ends. The earlier versions of 'Your Mother Should Know', 'The Fool on the Hill' and 'Glass Onion' arguably have the same, if not more, merit than the finished.

Elsewhere, beyond rejected songs such as the thrilling 'Leave My Kitten Alone' and the Decca Sessions material (see page 33), much here is of only passing interest. (See also Rejected songs page 150)

ANY TIME AT ALL
Words: Lennon Music: Lennon/McCartney
Recorded in 11 takes on 2nd June 1964
Found on *A Hard Day's Night*

John here gives a towering vocal to a lyric that simply does not deserve it. Writing speedily for a three-day schedule in the studio just before a worldwide tour, he rehashed two of his older songs. The opening bars to 'Anytime At All' and 'It Won't Be Long' both repeat the title three times, before explaining why John will soon be with the person to whom he is singing. Similarly, 'Anytime At All' closely follows the third verse to 'All I've Got to Do', which encourages the listener to call him if in need. This obedience to ideas conveying a message of loyalty for a teen-girl fan base showed John at an impasse. Where he sounded sincere on 'From Me To You' and 'I Want To Hold Your Hand', his offer to try to keep the sun shining here is risible.

In the rush, John entered the studio without a middle section. Unable or perhaps unwilling to add anything to these over familiar words, Paul stepped in and improvised a haughty instrumental middle eight on piano.

ASK ME WHY

Lennon/McCartney
B-side to the 'Please Please Me' single
The only Beatles song John wrote that he did not publicly comment on.
Recorded on 26th November 1962
Found on *Please Please Me*

A mystery lyric. This is largely a tale of requited love until its pay-off line reveals the situation is 'misery'. Either John, who is the main writer, is playing a joke on the listener, which is entirely in character, or it is a mix of ideas that never properly gelled. The only sense is in the opening words, which show John in familiar conversational mode, drawing the listener into his world.

Written in response to Brian Epstein's request for new material for the group's first-ever trip to Abbey Road, its attention to detail appears an attempt at impressing George Martin, so that he would choose it as an A-side. In particular, its pretty guitar flourishes and elaborate vocal harmonies make it stand out from the plainer B-sides which followed ('Thank You Girl' and 'I'll Get You').

BABY'S IN BLACK

Lennon/McCartney
"The next song is a waltz", John announcing 'Baby's in Black' on stage.
Completed in 14 takes on 11th August 1964
Found on *Beatles For Sale*

In mischievous mood at the height of Beatlemania, John and Paul sat down to compose something that would not conform to the public's expectation. As Paul recalled, an unhappy ending was sought, at odds with the ebullience of the most popular Lennon/McCartney lyrics. An unusual time signature, somewhat reminiscent of a sea-shanty sung by homesick sailors was added, as well as the corny humour of singing of feeling 'blue' with a bluesy seventh chord underneath.

Inspiration came from an 18th century nursery rhyme 'Johnny So Long at the Fair', whose first line was 'Oh dear, what can the matter be'. The rhyme tells of a girl who is upset at 'Johnny', who has not returned from the fair with her presents. 'Baby's In Black', is written from the view of a third person, another boy, who is trying to convince the girl to see Johnny as a 'mistake' and to turn to him instead. Both make heavy use of colour imagery. The girl in the nursery rhyme bemoans the lack of blue ribbons she has not received for her brown hair, while John and Paul complain of feeling blue because their girl is wearing black.

The fun had in putting this together made it dear to both of them and it became a regular live number – a coded way of saying 'this one's for us'.

In the studio the boundary-breaking continued with Country and Western verses welded onto a signature of Beatles' pop, uplifting vocal harmonies set over minor chords. It seems likely the original idea was John's as he went on to use nursery rhymes as the basis for both 'All You Need Is Love' and 'Cry Baby Cry'.

BABY IT'S YOU

Written by Mack David/Luther Dixon/Burt Bacharach
Recorded in three takes on 11th February 1963
Found on *Please Please Me*

When singing live the Beatles' cover versions were often at variance to the original lyrics. Played continuously after the words had been scribbled down on soon to be lost scraps of paper, it is easy to see how they evolved through learnt mistakes. Here John's changes typify his positive outlook on life. The original by The Shirelles, ends with a repeat of the first verse with its tale of sitting alone at home in tears. However, John closes by repeating the second verse with its message of defiance, that despite what others say about his love cheating him, he will ignore them and there will never be another 'you'. The effect is electric – while Shirley Owens, The Shirelles' lead singer, is left alone and pitiful, John is a hero.

The endless hours in Hamburg and Liverpool were an education on how to draw out drama from songs not realised by their original performers. Where US artists under licence were often given newly-written material to record on the very day they entered the studio, the Beatles could explore the arrangement and the nuances of the words. Occasionally lyrics were just tidied up. So 'never, never, ever been true' replaces 'never, never, never been true' and likewise nights 'go by' instead of 'rolling by'.

One of the last recordings from the long day spent making *Please Please Me*, here John's voice delivers an enormous, passionate charge and his rhythm guitar drives the band. By contrast, The Shirelles' original, a US hit in February 1962, had Owens' heavily-echoed vocals plonked on a murky keyboard instrumental by Burt Bacharach.

BABY YOU'RE A RICH MAN

Lennon/McCartney
Recorded at Olympic Studios in South-West London – a studio
favoured by the Rolling Stones.
Recorded in 12 takes on May 11th 1967
Found on *Magical Mystery Tour*

Quickly knocked out, John's playing of a clavioline, a plastic battery-powered keyboard not only mocks the artificiality of the 'weekend hippies' who first felt his ire on 'Day Tripper', but scrawls all over a soulful performance led by Paul's syncopated piano chords. It would be a thrill to hear the track remixed without it. Perhaps it was the presence of Mick Jagger in the studio which resulted in caution at showing off how the group worked at their best. Speedily recorded, John's dreamy falsetto, minus any special effects, mimics the nirvana the hippies believe they have found. A popular theory about the chorus, written by Paul, is that it was about Brian Epstein's habit of receiving tour receipts in cash in a large paper bag. Many claim to hear the word 'jew' instead of 'too' sung by John in the free-for-all sing-along at the close.

BACK IN THE USSR

McCartney
The basic track was recorded on 22nd August 1968 with Paul on
drums, John on bass and George on guitar. Extensive overdubs were
made the following day.
Found on *The Beatles* aka The White Album

'Back In The USSR' and 'Revolution' were politically inspired lyrics written in India within weeks of each other and where Paul refers to himself obliquely as 'comrad', John uses the western revolutionary term 'brother'.

It is likely Paul struck first, as he had already gone to

India with the idea of lampooning a government campaign aimed at getting people to buy more British-produced goods to ease a trade deficit. The campaign had its own T-shirts, posters and a song with the lines 'We're all backing Britain. The feeling is growing, so let's keep it going, the good times are blowing our way'. Paul was not the only one to mock the campaign. The TV comedy sketch show *Do Not Adjust Your Set* used the punch-line 'I'm baking Britain' for one of its sketches from this year.

In the same absurd spirit, he imagined a patriotic lyric extolling the virtues of the USSR (the Russian-controlled union of communist states), then a pariah state. And then used Chuck Berry's 'Back In The USA' and the Beach Boys 'California Girls' as a musical template. For good measure the Beach Boys' tame description of US girls is put into a smuttier setting, with references to sloping mountains and 'Daddy's farm' and he sought to sing it with a Jerry Lee Lewis accent.

The exhilaratingly playing and wild guitar solos belie the crisis under which it was made. Completed after Ringo had walked out after facing criticism of the way he played drums, the shock of his exit encouraged the others to raise their game. The same could not be said of the sound quality which is noticeably murkier than the recent 'Hey Jude'/ 'Revolution' single, which makes it hard to believe George Martin played a role either.

BAD BOY

The Beatles recorded three songs written by Larry Williams ('Slow Down', 'Dizzy Miss Lizzie' and 'Bad Boy'), the Rolling Stones recorded one ('She Said Yeah').
Recorded in four takes on 10th May 1965
Found on *Past Masters*

Quickly churned out to help US label Capitol create a new

album of off-cuts – *Beatles VI*, John muddles his way through a lyric (0.15-0.17) that he has forgotten, while backing vocals are dispensed with. The Larry Williams original from 1958 features a backing singer intoning 'he's a bad boy' in a baritone voice, meaning that nowhere on the Beatles' cover is the title sung. The group's haste was due to resentment at how these US albums offered only 10 tracks, which represented poorer value than the ones in Europe which had 14.

THE BALLAD OF JOHN AND YOKO

Words: Lennon   Music: Lennon/McCartney
Single released 30th May 1969
Banned by US radio stations for its use of the word 'Christ' as a
profanity it only reached No.8 in the US charts
Recorded in one day on 14th April 1969
Found on *Past Masters*

Jesus Christ was an inspiration for John when he turned his honeymoon with Yoko Ono into a global campaign for peace. Interviewed in his hotel bed in Amsterdam, he said: "We're trying to make Christ's message contemporary. What would he have done if he'd had advertisements, records, films, TV and newspapers? Christ made miracles to tell his message. Well, the miracle today is communications, so let's use it."

The speculation within 'The Ballad of John and Yoko' that he would be crucified for this peace-keeping role makes for an extraordinary statement from a major pop star. And yet there is also boyish mischief. The word 'Christ' appears in its usage as an everyday profanity only three years after his 'the Beatles are bigger than Jesus Christ' comments.

The song also served as a wedding present to Yoko just as Paul's 'Two of Us' was a gift for Linda Eastman – both romanticise the couples' travels together. Stylistic inspiration came from Georgie Fame's recent hit 'The Ballad of Bonnie and Clyde'. John drew a parallel with the American bandits who played cat and mouse with the US press and authorities, criss-crossing state lines. He and Yoko were similarly pursued across Europe in March 1969 by journalists. Prepared quickly with the immediacy of a television news item, the thrill was in getting it released while John's marriage and peace campaign was still fresh in people's minds. With both George and Ringo out of the country, Paul remembered: '[John] came round to my house, wanting to do it really quick, he said "Let's just you and me run over to the studio". I said "Oh, all right, I'll play drums, I'll play bass".'

Starting from an unpromising E, E7, A, B chord progression, over a single day every trick was used to fill it out. The bass line (which came via Elvis Presley's 'Don't Be Cruel') is pushed high for a counter-melody, a decorative guitar figure (this is a musical joke, being derived from 'The Honeymoon Song' by Marino Marini and his Quartet) is added, piano seeps into the cracks, Paul's vocal shadows John's, the drums are highly echoed and on the last verse maracas appear.

The speed with which it was written laid bare its sources. The closing riff is from Johnny Burnette's 'Lonesome Tears In My Eyes' while the verse rhythm is loosely based on Chuck Berry's 'Johnny B Goode'. Tellingly when Berry explains to the listener that Louisiana is a place close to New Orleans, John tells us Gibraltar, where he went to get married, is near Spain.

The other Beatles could not have been thrilled about promoting a relationship that was tearing them apart and having their brand exploited to publicise John's idiosyncratic campaign. However, this was the price paid for avoiding the tension already caused by their veto of 'Revolution' a year before. Indeed, John seems to have backed off from creating too much conflict on the making of *Abbey Road* as recompense.

BEATLES FOR SALE
Recorded in 36 hours, mixed in 15 hours
Album released 4th December 1964

The thousand-yard stares on the cover reveal the fatigue of a non-stop, ten month cash-in on Beatlemania. From January to the end of October 1964 the Beatles recorded 36 songs for two albums, two singles and a four-track EP. They made one feature film, did countless TV appearances, numerous interviews and a one-off TV special. There were 11 nights of pantomime in London, tours of Britain, Australia, New Zealand, North America (twice), plus additional ad hoc gigs in the UK, Denmark, the Netherlands and Hong Kong. One part of their American schedule took them from Quebec to Florida and then back up to Boston in four days.

The schedule was dictated by the unfounded fear that success might evaporate and the pressure encouraged a rabid partying that further took its toll. By several accounts the scenes in hotels post-concert on the Australian and US tours were the most debauched of their career. By the autumn, when the cover picture was shot, the group were, quite simply, running on empty.

Beatles For Sale was made towards the end of this mad schedule, fitted in gaps from a UK tour. With little prepared, space was filled with three-chord cover versions which could be knocked out in one take. In one marathon session six songs were recorded. Weariness brought a jaded and mocking tone. Neither 'I Feel Fine' nor 'She's A Woman' takes itself seriously and after the feedback on 'I Feel Fine' someone off-mic can be heard muttering the word 'shit'. 'Baby's In Black', 'I'm A Loser' and 'I Don't

Want to Spoil the Party' subvert the upbeat themes of earlier songs. Their heavy work-load is alluded to on 'Eight Days a Week' and 'What You're Doing' and the album title is itself a comment on their commercial exploitation. Some of this attitude is traceable to the acerbic lyrics of Bob Dylan and an anaemic use of acoustic guitar replaces the big wash of electric guitar. The lightness of sound this results in may not just have been a stylistic move, but more a craving for a quieter life after the screams and frenzy of their tours.

BECAUSE

Words: Lennon   Music: Lennon/McCartney
The last new song the Beatles recorded
The basic track was recorded on 1st August 1969, the vocals on 4th August and the moog synthesiser 5th August
Found on *Abbey Road*

John's description of a universal love, which is 'you', 'new' and 'all', followed days after Paul sang about the love we make being equal to the love we take. John declared Paul's line on 'The End' as 'cosmic' and only days after the transmission of pictures of the earth and moon by Apollo 9 during the first moon landing in July 1969 his words also refer to the earth, the sky and the wind. This all-encompassing love is evoked in the complex and painstaking three-part harmonies. These can be heard as an an elegy for the Beatles too, as it was their last group performance, but it is more likely one-upmanship, after the sensation caused by the dreamy three-part harmonies on the debut Crosby Still & Nash album that summer.

John said the main arpeggio had been lifted from Beethoven's 'Moonlight Sonata', though the notes are identical to the riff on 'I Want You [She's So Heavy]' (listen to the first 10 seconds and then skip forward to the intro of 'Because' on *Abbey Road*). The classical theme was extended to the use of synthesiser, George's playing mimics the tone of French horns giving a regal, sci-fi reading, that again recalls the moon landing.

BEING FOR THE BENEFIT OF MR KITE
Lennon/McCartney
"Messrs Kite and Henderson in announcing the following entertainments assure the public that this night's productions will be one of the most splendid ever produced in this town having been some days in preparation." Words from the 1843 circus poster owned by John.
The basic track was recorded on 17th February 1967 with overdubs on 20th February and 29th March 1967
Found on *Sgt. Pepper's Lonely Hearts Club Band*

What would a song advertising a circus in 1843 sound like? This is the exciting premise John and Paul set themselves when bringing to life an antique poster describing the attractions of a circus in Rochdale, Lancashire. They settled on a keyboard and a strict beat and chord pattern, as befitting music recorded in an era before rock'n'roll, blues or jazz. In this starchy Victorian setting, the band, the announcer informs us, starts promptly at ten minutes to six. The tone recalls the Master of Ceremonies impersonated on the album's intro a week before. It also echoes the tone of 'When I'm 64' with a request for a loved one to 'indicate' everything 'precisely'. Indeed, it seems likely that John bought the poster with the intention of using it as source material to fit with these songs. Meanwhile, the chords lurch from major to minor and back again as if mimicking an elephant ambling through a circus ring. The only break from this rigidity comes from their head-masterly producer, George Martin, who out of character plays the swirling melody line on harmonium and adds the nightmarish steam organ solo too. The latter was made up of several tapes cut up and stuck together randomly – an effect that left John ecstatic on hearing it for the first time.

However, his views changed. In early 1968 he told Beatles' biographer, Hunter Davies: "I didn't dig that song when I wrote it. I didn't believe in it when we were recording it. But nobody will believe it. They don't want to. They want it to be important." He was resentful at the way he had become answerable to the success of *Sgt. Pepper's*, an album for which he largely ceded creative control. In 1970, when interviewed for Rolling Stone newspaper, he cited the song as sticking to what he described as Paul's 'come and see the show' idea.

John was also irritated at interpretations of the lyrics, many seeing the dancing horse as a reference to drugs – 'horse' being slang for heroin. Embarrassed, he sought to scotch these rumours by being photographed standing next to the Victorian circus poster to make his point. The poster is revealing of how much he drew upon its words and styling – only changing the horse's name from 'Zanthus' to 'Henry'. Notably, where it uses capital letters to make a point e.g. 'THE WORLD', 'REAL FIRE' John exclaims these words.

BIRTHDAY

Words: McCartney/Lennon   Music: McCartney/Lennon/Harrison
Neither John nor Paul recorded a single note of Beatles' music on their birthdays (John's birthday was on 9th October, Paul's is 18th June), though George and Ringo did.
Recorded in one through the night session 18th-19th September 1968
Found on *The Beatles* aka The White Album

Deceptively simple, over two minutes and 39 seconds this track actually fits in seven sections, all with their own texture. The opening riff and crack of snare drum is filched from Roy Orbison's 'Pretty Woman'. This is followed by the revved-up drum and tambourine interlude, then comes John's 'party, party' chord-driven refrain and the call and response vocal led by Paul with backing from Patti Boyd and Yoko Ono. Next is the re-introduction of the main riff with a distorted piano backing, a spiky lead guitar break and finally, the closing distorted piano notes. Written and recorded in a single evening, Paul started whilst waiting for the others to arrive. After a break to watch an old rock'n'roll film on TV, *The Girl Can't Help It*, they returned with lyrics that suggest the foggy glow of either alcohol – the refrain of 'happy birthday' comes across as more of a drunken threat than a celebration.

BLACKBIRD

Words: McCartney/Lennon   Music: McCartney
Written partly as an exercise of creating a tricky finger picked melody on guitar
"I had in mind a black woman, rather than a bird", Paul '98
Recorded in 32 takes on 11th June 1968
Found on *The Beatles* aka The White Album

Paul explained 'Blackbird' as a message of hope to the American black civil rights movement, but the ability of anyone to identify with its call for strength in hard times is what makes it popular. Indeed, it makes more sense as a message written for himself. He was suffering the breakdown (a 'black night') of his partnership with John and the sudden end of his long-term relationship with Jane Asher. This isolation is evoked by its skilful guitar picking, which replicates the sound of two musicians. It would seem that he was not fully convinced of his message of hope; where he sings the word 'arise' the tune is actually descending.

BLUE JAY WAY

Harrison
The basic track was recorded 6th September 1967 with overdubs on 7th
September and 6th October
Found on *Magical Mystery Tour*

Wonderfully foreboding, the first two lines to 'Blue Jay Way' are like a tale of impending horror for George's friends who are lost in the fog. Starting with the eeriest single note on a keyboard, the entrance of a thudding, relentless beat evokes the violence awaiting his friends or the thudding of their hearts, while the downward chord pattern and George's disembodied voice all make for chilling effect. The fog is also, inescapably, a nod to the altered states achieved on drugs and not just a comment on the local weather in Los Angeles where he was staying in a rented house. The same can be said for the backwards tapes and the vari-speeded instruments. This fine introduction does not deliver on its promise and a wearying use of repetition hints at madness and indicates, as the lyrics state, someone who has lost their way. George's mood when writing was intensified by his recent visit to the hippie haven, Haight-Ashbury, in San Francisco. Rather than the bold new love generation, in his eyes he saw only decay and dereliction.

BOYS

Written by Luther Dixon and Wes Farrell
Recorded in one take on 11th February 1963
Found on *Please Please Me*

Close your eyes and listen and you can not only hear the Beatles' Cavern sound here, but visualise their stage show too. To make up for the lead singer being hidden behind his cymbals and drums, John and Paul whoop and scream for extra impact.

The reason Ringo was singing a song written for a woman tells of the need for any group to have an original live act in Hamburg and Liverpool. While waiting to go on stage, to their horror the Beatles often heard the band prior to them playing their repertoire. As insurance they sought out covers of obscure or overlooked singles unlikely to be tackled by their rivals. 'Boys' was originally a slow and sultry B-side to 'Will You Still Love Me Tomorrow?' by The Shirelles, a hit in 1960. Here it is revved up into a wild rocker, without changing the lyrics gender for the chorus, (though the verses are changed), as Paul remembered for a "laugh". For a group used to playing in Europe's biggest red light district, such risqué behaviour was par for the course. Whether Ringo, who inherited 'Boys' from Pete Best, found this funny too is not documented.

CAN'T BUY ME LOVE

McCartney/ Lennon
The only Beatles' single recorded outside London at the EMI studios in Paris.
Released on 16th March 1964
Paul's scream before the guitar solo replicates Little Richard's scream on 'Tutti Frutti'.
Recorded in four takes on 29th January 1964
Found on *A Hard Day's Night*

Booked into the five-star Georges Cinq Hotel in Paris, while playing three weeks at the prestigious L'Olympia venue, Paul wrote a lyric showing his disaffection with the opulence and jewellery shops which surrounded him. To him Paris was a city of free, uninhibited love rather than wealth. Notably, John fondly recalled the group's stay for his memory of the sight of lovers kissing under the bridges over the Seine.

Paul's preference was for modesty in his dwellings too. Where John, George and Ringo bought large houses in

Surrey, his base for nearly two years was a small bedroom at his girlfriend's house in central London, almost as if he believed a life of luxury would harm his creativity.

Bohemian was also the keynote in the Beatles' adjoining suites at the George Cinq, with Bob Dylan's *Freewheelin'* album never far from the record turntable. The way the listener is addressed as 'my friend' on 'Blowin In The Wind' is repeated here.

That these deep thoughts were paired with a carefree melody is best explained by the incredible news that 'I Want to Hold Your Hand' was soaring up the US charts. The impromptu party thrown in Paris, when it eventually made No.1, they recalled as one of their happiest-ever moments. 'Can't Buy Me Love' came to be recorded in Paris, too, after a quick response was demanded by EMI after 'I Want To Hold Your Hand' was displaced from the UK No.1 spot. In the rush, unwittingly Paul created a formula that enabled the group to write to order. The use of three major chords for the verses and just two minor chords for the chorus achieves economical, but powerful drama and contrast. It was repeated on 'A Hard Day's Night', 'I Feel Fine' and 'I'm A Loser'.

CARRY THAT WEIGHT See page 56 (Golden Slumbers/ Carry That Weight)

CHAINS
Written by Gerry Goffin and Carole King
Recorded in four takes on 11th February 1963
Found on *Please Please Me*

'Chains' by the Cookies reached only No.30 in the UK charts in January 1963, but for fans of black R 'n' B it would have held far greater cachet. By covering a record from the New York girl group while it was still being played on the radio, the Beatles were making a statement on where their tastes and influences lay. The Cookies' original is distinguished by a sassy arrangement of handclaps, saxophones, guitars and drums, however, not having the chance to hone it live, this version is woefully Spartan. John and George simply play the same rhythm chords on a marginally faster arrangement, whilst adding an incongruous Arabic sounding harmonica motif which does not feature on the original.

COME TOGETHER

Words: Lennon Music: Lennon/McCartney
"One of my favourite Beatles' tracks" John '80
Released as a single 6th October 1969
The basic track was recorded on 21st July 1969 with overdubs on 22nd, 25th, 29th and 30th July
Found on *Abbey Road*

'Come!' Lead singers of rock bands have dreamed up many imaginative ways to alert guitarists to the point at which their solo should start: Little Richard would scream, whilst on the 1962 hit 'Louie Louie', the Kingsmen's lead singer memorably urged his guitarist to 'let 'em have it'. Here John's choice of word suggests the solo acts as a release of musical tension and also evokes the orgasm alluded to in the title. In his obsession for Yoko Ono, sex represented their union and these lyrics show the same lack of inhibition displayed in his erotic lithographs of the two of them. This desire to shock was a product of its times. Relaxation of theatre censorship laws in 1968 allowed nudity and swear words in London theatres, which the productions of *Oh Calcutta* and *Hair* capitalised on. Around this time too, Serge Gainsbourg and Jane Birkin recorded the equally shocking, 'Je t'aime..moi non plus', which featured a suggestive climax not a million miles from John's call before the guitar solo. While 'Je t'aime..moi non plus' was banned, 'Come Together' was not, as the lyrics, as John admitted are largely 'gobbledegook'.

It had not started this way. John had made a wayward promise to write a campaign song for Timothy Leary's bid to be elected as governor of California. Leary had the phrase 'come together' to which was added the line about people having to be free. This mission went astray the minute Chuck Berry's 'You Can't Catch Me' was used to fashion a metre for the verses. The first line is lifted straight and where Berry's lyrics display a fetish for the paraphernalia of US cars (air-mobile, souped-up jitney, hideaway wings, flight de ville), John used his own cool, impenetrable slang. What probably did survive of the attempt to write a campaign song is the word 'he' at the start of many lines, as if to describe Leary's attributes and campaign promises.

This gobbledegook was given grandeur after John sought a way of disguising the Chuck Berry influence (though he was still sued for plagiarism). Paul excelled himself, coming up with the sexy bass line and the Hammond organ part, and he no doubt had a hand in directing Ringo to play the peculiar drum pattern too. In his solo career, John would work with many talented musicians, but he never again had a collaborator who was capable of transforming his ideas in this way.

John's in put to the arrangement was influenced by drugs. The closing blissful moans and beautiful clear guitar notes that accompany them have an uncanny parallel to his solo recording of 'Cold Turkey' which closes with ugly distorted guitar notes and tortured screeches. Between the two songs John had forced himself off heroin and as such they make an unusual pairing, as the evocation of a heroin high and the horror of withdrawal.

CRY BABY CRY

Lennon

The lyrics mention Kirkaldy, a town on the east coast of Scotland which has no record of ever having a Duke or Duchess. The Beatles played there on Sunday 6th October 1963 and the lyric possibly alludes to someone John met during his stay.

The lyrics owe something to the 18th century nursery rhyme 'Sing a song of sixpence', particularly the verse "The king was in his counting house, counting out his money; the queen was in the parlour, eating bread and honey." Indeed this verse intrigued John so much he repeated it on his 1980 track 'Clean Up Time'.

Basic track recorded 16th July 1968 with overdubs on 18th July

Found on *The Beatles* aka The White Album

Revisiting the fantasia of 'Lucy in The Sky with Diamonds', John here leads the listener into an other-worldly tale of nonsense and whimsy. His vocals, featuring the best of his trademark cross rhythms and alliteration, are entirely convincing but, unlike 'Lucy', the backing is threadbare, its recording coming at an all time low in band relations. Chief engineer, Geoff Emerick, walked out during this session, unable to face any more of the snide remarks and paranoia. As evidence of this there are no harmony vocals and where Paul's input into 'Lucy' had been a bass line with a counter-melody, an extraordinary accented keyboard, and the writing of the chorus, here he merely plays a subdued bass – John's piano is perfunctory by comparison. Failing to match the alchemy of 'Lucy', its lyrics are left naked. Embarrassed, John later flippantly dubbed the track 'garbage'.

CRY FOR A SHADOW

Recorded 22nd June 1961 at the Frederick-Ebert-Halle, Hamburg, Germany

Credited to John and George, John created a chord pattern over which George fashioned the lead lines.

First released in August 1961

Found on *Anthology*

Recorded at a time when John and Paul were not writing anything as worthy as their club repertoire this became George's first and only B-side for the next seven years. As the Star Club tapes from December 1962 reveal, his role as the lead instrumentalist in a rock 'n' roll covers band was, for the time being, at least the equal of John and Paul. Created as light relief from the slog of Hamburg, George wanted to fool fellow Liverpudlians abroad, Rory Storm and The Hurricanes (who then had Ringo as a drummer), that it was actually the latest Shadows' release.

The string-bending extravaganza was released by Polydor in Germany as the B-side to 'My Bonnie', which was sung by Tony Sheridan with the Beatles as his backing group.

A DAY IN THE LIFE
Lennon/McCartney
Tara Browne's father was a titled aristocrat and, as the lyrics imply, neither John nor Paul was sure if this made him eligible for a seat in the House of Lords in London.
John wrote it on a piano with a newspaper propped up in front of him – Paul helped finish these verses.
The words to the backwards chant are apparently 'It really couldn't be any other.'
Basic track recorded on 19th January with overdubs on 20th January, 3rd and 10th February and the orchestral parts on 22nd February 1967
Found on *Sgt.Pepper's Lonely Hearts Club Band*

John's elegy to a friend who had died weeks before not only stunned listeners on release, but all who first heard it. Its regally-echoed vocals with their tale of a life cut short filled band-mates and studio staff with awe. Paul's piano and Ringo's drums skirt gingerly around the loaded words, being delicate when John sings and loud when he pauses. Even then, the tone was deemed too harsh by chief engineer, Geoff Emerick, who loosened the drum skins to give a booming gravitas.

Awe was what John was sought. In a shocking contrast, he requested a sound like the world ending to cap these verses. Paul, who was nurturing an interest in classical music, suggested an orchestra, no doubt aware of the power of pieces such as Gustav Holst's *Mars, the Bringer of War* from his *Planets Suite* but also keen to try his luck in the avant-garde style of John Cage. Members of the Royal Philharmonic and the London Symphony Orchestra were duly conscripted to bring alive his idea of each instrument discordantly starting from its lowest note to its highest in order to create the nightmare John sought. The 40 musicians were also employed to give the imperious chords (2.50-3.19) that help place John's cries as calling down from heaven. The person who months before had contemplated quitting after the backlash at his 'the Beatles are bigger than Jesus Christ' comments, was back as provocative as ever, though it was the linking of death with the LSD experience which saw 'A Day in the Life' banned by the BBC.

Tara Browne, a rich 21-year old socialite in London, had been dead barely a month when John put pen to paper. An acquaintance of the group, he had been with Paul when he first took LSD in early 1966 and the language of a drugs trip is used to describe his fatal head injuries in a car crash that December. The key falsetto phrase uttered about turning us on – actually Paul's idea – is invoking the listener into the LSD brotherhood John enjoyed among his circle of friends such as Browne. There is a cold detachment – he even admits to laughing, or laughing 'half' as he corrects himself mid-word – but this admittance of an inappropriate response is beautifully sung it as if for a requiem. Similarly, his apparently uncaring mixture of banal and tragic images serves to tell of everyday life carrying on regardless; the holes in the road in Blackburn came from a news-in-brief item from the same newspaper in which Browne's death was reported. While the final massed piano chord in its abruptness not only makes a fitting end to the album, but conjures up the finality of death.

Always cautious of being taken too seriously, or perhaps of having his lyrics taken too literally, John allowed in a piece of light. A gap for a middle eight was left for Paul to fill. His breezy, upbeat recollection of running to catch the bus as a teenager and then taking a smoke, (marijuana is inferred), fits like the illogical twist of events in a dream.

DAY TRIPPER
Lennon/McCartney
A double A-side single with 'We Can Work It Out' released
3rd December 1965
Recorded on 16th October 1965
Found on *Past Masters*

The three distorted guitar notes on '(I Can't Get No) Satisfaction' make up the most famous riff in rock 'n' roll and on its release the Rolling Stones status soared. Stung into action, only two months later the Beatles were recording an emphatic response. John no doubt spent days working on this adopting 'I Feel Fine's trick of taking a standard blues riff and adding a flourish of melodic notes. Bo Diddley's 'Road Runner', which he regularly played live from 1961-62 uses the same opening notes and it is also has a put-down lyric about a woman, that uses travel as a euphemism. Like 'Satisfaction', 'Day Tripper' follows a theme of sexual frustration, complaining of a woman who will not, or cannot, consummate their relationship. It was a private boast of Jagger's that he had managed to slip in a hidden reference to menstruation ('losing streak'). Similarly, where Paul first sings of a girl being a big 'teaser', the phrase is barely imperceptibly repeated as 'prick teaser'. How many other hidden references there are is a moot point. The trip is of course LSD, while the girl who 'plays' at one-night stands and the act of 'taking' an easy way out probably had some meaning to the Beatles in-crowd. Paul recalled in *Many Years From Now*: "We were interested in winking to our friends and comrades in arms, putting in references that we knew our friends would get but that the Great British Public might not."

John had to fight for this to be made an A-side, perhaps as the rest of the band was uncomfortable at following the Stones. Reviewers and the public preferred 'We Can Work It Out', but fellow musicians gave the thumbs up to 'Day Tripper' with both Jimi Hendrix and Otis Redding recording it. While sonically exciting, the speed with which it was mixed is revealed at 1.50 and at 2.32 where sound levels change clumsily for the drop-in of overdubbed vocals.

DEAR PRUDENCE

Lennon
Paul plays drums and bass
Basic track recorded 28th August 1968 with overdubs the following day.
Found on *The Beatles* aka The White Album

John's message to enjoy the simpler things in life has an appeal beyond its initial purpose. Written to lure Prudence, the sister of film star Mia Farrow, out of her bungalow in India after weeks of her relentless meditation worried fellow students, John set about his task by pointing out all that she was missing. His own house bound, drug induced seclusion 1966-67 must have provided inspiration. The simple beauty of the melody suggests the delicate nature of the task for which it was intended, its soft drone note gives a steady reassurance that no harm was meant. John's sincerity is clear too in the absence of any surreal or sardonic asides.

THE DECCA AUDITION

Recorded 1st January 1962 at Decca Studios, Broadhurst Gardens in North London
Only five of the 15 Decca tracks were officially released on *Anthology 1* in 1995.

Common theories on why the Decca sessions disappoint tend to remove the Beatles from blame. There is the excuse of having to play in a cold strange studio on 1st January, the weakness of Pete Best's drumming, being subjected to Brian Epstein's playlist and Decca's general inability to spot the presence of greatness underneath their noses. In truth, no one is blameless. John and Paul's vocals are affected by nerves, there are little of the chiming vocal harmonies that adorn their first few singles, while George has not yet learnt how to properly match a solo to a song. In fairness to them, the situation was alien and intimidating. By the sound of it they had been instructed to limit their volume. The worst effected is the normally boisterous John, their nominal leader, who is audibly nervous on 'Money', docile on 'To Know Her Is To Love Her', lacking authority on 'Memphis Tennessee' and unconvincing on 'Hello Little Girl'. Paul gives a rousing 'Searchin' and a fair rendition of 'Till There Was You', but is all fake charm on 'September In The Rain', unremarkable on 'Sure To Fall' and 'Besame Mucho', while 'Love of the Loved' is over-wrought. Only George was immune to nerves, tackling the gawky lyrics of 'The Sheik of Araby', 'Three Cool Cats' and 'Take Good Care of My Baby' with relish.

Decca's rejection must have been crushing, but ultimately it spurred them on. In between the audition in January and the recording of 'Please Please Me' in November, they played almost nightly, learning and improving as they went. Meanwhile Decca, chose Brian Poole and the Tremeloes, as, so legend would have it, the London-based group's travel costs would have been less.

DEVIL IN HER HEART

Written by Richard Drapkin
Recorded in six takes on 18th July 1963
Found on *With the Beatles*

Unearthing hidden gems from obscure r'n'b records, was an everyday task for British beat bands of the early Sixties and the practice of re-arranging each of them for two guitars, bass and harmony vocals acted as a song-writing master class. 'Devil in *His* Heart' would have been one of the last of 400-500 cover versions learnt before the Beatles became recording artists in the autumn of 1962 and their arrangement is exemplary. Where on the original, the guitar riff is pinched and faltering, George delivers a grand flourish before the vocals' entrance. There is a move up-tempo too, for greater urgency, so much so that it is 13 seconds shorter than the original. This is clear in the rapid interplay of Paul's vocals, which warn George of the ill intentions of his loved one. It is likely the visual impact of this exchange of views was more important as a new live number than for its eventual impact on vinyl. The Donays were three female singers from Detroit whose recording of 'Devil in His Heart' featured a shrill, off-pitch lead vocal and failed to chart. The Beatles only heard it as their manager, Brian Epstein, had a policy of seeking to stock every single on UK release at his record store in Liverpool.

DIG A PONY

Lennon
Recorded live on a rooftop in Savile Row, London 30th January 1969
Found on *Let It Be*

In its first rehearsals this was entitled 'All I Want Is You', but John lost patience and derisively renamed it 'Dig a Pony'. Possibly its similarity to Bob Dylan's 'I Want You' bothered him. It uses the same device of a simple message of desire contrasted with convoluted and near meaningless verses. In this way he is saying the only message that counts is his, some would say unhealthy, desire for Yoko. John must have discussed this as out-takes of the *Let It Be* sessions reveal snatches of 'I Want You' played during rehearsals.

He uses his nonsense verse to smuggle in some cheeky comments – (Dylan does the same on 'I Want You'). His poke at the Rolling Stones imitating 'everyone' they know is his way of letting off steam at their *Beggars Banquet* album using a plain white sleeve a month after the release of *The White Album*.

The performance of 'Dig a Pony' is from the rooftop concert in Savile Row, London – turn up the last few seconds and you can hear John complain that his hands are too cold to play the guitar.

DIG IT
Lennon/McCartney/Harrison/Starr/Preston
Recorded in one take on 26th January 1969
Found on *Let It Be*

At school John would entertain his classmates by drawing caricatures of his teachers and this is a similar response at being marshalled into a project he was losing enthusiasm for. From a 12 minute jam, the 1 minute 20 second edit mocks Bob Dylan's more abstruse lyrics and uses a chord arrangement similar to 'Like a Rolling Stone'. While once a disciple, John's affections for Dylan had waned; he had already parodied him on 'I Am the Walrus' and would do so years later on 'You've Got To Serve Somebody'. Another influence is 'Initials' from the musical *Hair*, which creates a satire around the acronyms FBI, CIA as well as LSD and LBJ (Lyndon Johnson, president of the USA 1963-1969). Paul, in his biography, claimed that all four

Beatles added ideas, hence the equal writing credit, though as Billy Preston also played, perhaps he should be credited too.

DIZZY MISS LIZZIE

Written by Larry Williams
Recorded in two takes on the morning of 10th May 1965
Found on *Help!*

John liked singing early rock 'n' roll more for the physical thrill he got in performing it, than for fretting over whether he got the words right and none of his recordings of 'Dizzy Miss Lizzie' is the same. On the album *Help!* he repeats the second verse at the end and at one point mis-sings 'Dizzy dizz lizzie'. The BBC radio version from this year misses the final verse and the even rustier version from *Live Peace in Toronto* forgets the third and fourth verses. Despite John's obvious enthusiasm, this number would have been sharper back in 1962 when it was being played regularly live and this is an overblown two minutes 52 seconds compared to the succinct Larry Williams original at two minutes 12 seconds.

DON'T BOTHER ME

Words: Harrison   Music: Harrison/Lennon/McCartney
Written whilst ill in bed
Seven takes were made on 11th September 1963, but the next day the group recorded afresh with a new arrangement completed in nine takes.
Found on *With the Beatles*

Whereas John and Paul sang please, and thank you, and offered loving arms to woo the group's new fans, here George told them to go away. Locked out of their hit-writing partnership he was unfettered by commercial necessities and his downbeat mood is a break from jollity and true love sentiments. If the lyrics were true to him it is debatable how much of the music is. In a fractious business meeting from 1969, John reproached George for his claim that he had been side-lined over the course of their career and cited the help given on 'Don't Bother Me'. "I remember the riff you were playing", he recalled, which suggests it was re-worked, as there is no riff in the finished recording. The sweet plaintive breaks from the downbeat verses reveals the fine touch of Lennon/McCartney and John's hurt suggests that he and Paul had a right to a credit.

DON'T LET ME DOWN

Lennon
B-side to 'Get Back'
The sentiments are identical to 'If I Fell'.
Recorded on 28th January 1969
Found on *Past Masters*

An expressive voice, experienced musicians and a change in time signature can all bring alive a three-chord song, as this extraordinary performance shows. John's voice turns from anguished on the chorus, to gentle on the verses to uplifting on the middle eight. All the more real for being played in the live, stripped-down style of the *Let It Be* project; the points where his voice breaks and glitches in sound levels occur merely add to its authenticity. The lasting impact is of soul music at its best.

The arrangement evolved over nine days of rehearsals allowing the virtuoso instrumental breaks to be perfected. Billy Preston, who plays the Hammond organ solo, came from a blues and gospel background and the way his notes answer the vocals is a revelation. Suitably impressed, John sought to make him a permanent member of the band.

John later defended the lyrics from the criticism that their simplicity showed a decline in his talent. On the contrary, he argued their directness and honesty were, if anything, progress. Paul later interpreted them as being not just about John's love (and lust) for Yoko Ono, but also his fear over the heroin use they were indulging in. Intrigued, Paul adapted its unusual turn of phrase for describing what his lover does for him – she 'does me/it good' – for his solo career highlight, 'My Love'.

DON'T PASS ME BY

Words: Starkey   Music: Starkey/McCartney
A basic track of piano and drums was recorded on 5th June 1968 with overdubs on 6th June, 12th, 22nd July
Found on *The Beatles* aka The White Album

Ringo describes waiting for a loved one to arrive, a clock ticking and the anticipation of footsteps coming down a path. Endlessly hanging around when making *the White Album* he was frequently in the studio reception reading newspapers and magazines and after one interminable wait he snapped after facing criticism of his playing from Paul and stormed out for two weeks.

John and George are absent here and Paul took charge of the music to create a hokey, offbeat charm, which does not give the lyrics any unwarranted gloss. His layers of piano, keyboard and guitars are the main accompaniment to the drums and vocals.

The origins of 'Don't Pass Me By' stretch back as far as 1963, when Ringo mentioned that he had started a song of the same name.

DO YOU WANT TO KNOW A SECRET?

Lennon/McCartney
George was not given enough time and was unhappy with his vocal.
Recorded in eight takes on 11th February 1963
Found on *Please Please Me*

'Listen!', the use of an imperative word or phrase is a characteristic start for a John Lennon lyric. While the true-love themes of his early lyrics pandered to the hit parade, his desire to reach out to people was genuine, even if, as here, the lyrics ultimately did not make a great deal of sense.

A patchwork of ideas, the opening line is lifted from 'You'll Never Know', a song popularised by Frank Sinatra and Vera Lynn, while the line 'Want to know a secret? Promise not to tell?' had been sung to him by his mother. She had heard it in 'I'm Wishing' in the Walt Disney cartoon *Snow White and the Seven Dwarfs*. This leaves George singing that a girl will never know how much he loves her, then confusingly, that both of them have known the secret of their love for a couple of weeks. John and Paul seem to mock his predicament in bringing this nonsense to life; their inane scat harmonies on the second verse provoke a barely concealed snigger from George (0.48). Naturalistic wails and whoops reveal this as a song they had got to know live between writing in September 1962 and recording in February. The only performance from the *Please Please Me* album to rely on the use of acoustic guitar, the clipped way John plays the chords is reminiscent of a French love song.

DOCTOR ROBERT
Lennon/McCartney
The instruments were recorded on 17th April 1966, the vocals on 19th April.
Found on *Revolver*

'John's tribute to the medical profession', was how Britain's weekly paper, the New Musical Express described this in its review of *Revolver*. It was in fact a mischievous prank on anyone gormless enough to think of it that way. John, according to his close friend Pete Shotton, delighted in the thought that his fans would sing along unaware that it was about a notorious New York doctor whose vitamin shots were mixed with narcotics. The joke would have been a source of private amusement in the Beatles' circle of widely-travelled rock star friends and reflects the growing interest John took in distorting his public image. In the same spirit he ditched the clever chord sequences he had often slaved over. The verses stick to the key of A for a full 18 seconds before shifting to F# for almost as long.

DRIVE MY CAR

Music: McCartney   Words: McCartney/Lennon
"Drive My Car was an old blues euphemism for sex", Paul '98
Recorded in one day on 13th October 1965
Found on *Rubber Soul*

The woman here, a 'bitch' in Paul's recollection, bears a resemblance to the pretty and conniving character played by Julie Christie in the film *Darling*. She rises from nothing to become a fashion model, before marrying into nobility and ending up a somewhat lost and unhappy celebrity. The film, which was on general release when 'Drive My Car' was made, was a landmark of Sixties' cinema for its portrayal of a permissive, socially mobile demi-monde and it is hard to imagine that John and Paul were unaware of it.

Paul's first lyrics were about a girl 'on the make' in Los Angeles, who asks her boyfriend to buy her 'golden rings'. Recoiling from this clumsy first draft, he sought help from John who came up with the loaded and intriguing suggestion that the girl should drive his car. This may well refer to John's reliance on a chauffeur after a series of car smashes. As a lyric it was clever if not soulful and the music is likewise. The weld of jazz, soul and rock is a showcase for Paul's growing virtuosity. He plays the distorted guitar solo, the strutting bass and the syncopated piano chords. Summing up this brimming confidence, the vocal harmonies use beeping car horn noises to echo the lyrics' theme, which owes something to the harmony vocals on Bo Diddley's 'Road Runner'.

EIGHT DAYS A WEEK
Music: McCartney   Words: McCartney/Lennon
The first time a whole day was devoted to recording a Beatles' song (6th October 1964). The opening riff was added on 18th October 1964
Found on *Beatles For Sale*

How far can a song be improved by studio production alone? This intriguing task led to seven hours being devoted to 'Eight Days a Week', a miniscule amount by today's standards, but a huge expanse of time then, three hours having been the Beatles' previous limit. Time was used to create the first fade-in for a pop record, a 12-string guitar riff, handclaps to heighten urgency and the dramatic moment where all instruments stop except for the bass when John and Paul sing 'I lu-uh-uh-uh-ve you'. That this went to No.1 in the USA shows the effort paid off, but the process had stretched John's patience. Reminiscing some 16 years later, he tetchily recalled a struggle to perfect, at Paul's bidding, what he described as a 'lousy' song. Notably, this trite declaration of an enduring love has none of the emotional depth of 'Things We Said Today' and 'No Reply' from this year. The title was an accurate description of the Beatles' workload and came from an expression Paul heard his equally-overworked chauffeur use.

ELEANOR RIGBY
Music: McCartney   Words: McCartney/Lennon
"When I was a kid there was this old lady in Gambier Terrace...I always used to feel sorry for her, an old spinster lady living on her own...in my mind she became the prototype for Eleanor Rigby." Paul '99
Single released 5th August 1966

The strings were recorded on 28th April 1966 the vocals on 29th April and 6th June
Found on *Revolver*

It is perhaps the most powerful pop song to depict a funeral, but 'Eleanor Rigby' was not the first. In fact, when it was written, a song about a funeral was at No.1 in the charts. Whilst not obvious to the casual listener, the Rolling Stones' 'Paint It Black' obliquely refers to the death of a girlfriend who is carried off in a cortege of black cars with tinted windows, with flowers strewn over her coffin. Given that Paul had a strategic partnership with Mick Jagger to ensure the release dates of their singles were kept apart, Paul was certainly no casual listener. Temporarily, it seems, both bands were competing to write the best songs about death.

Paul already had a mordant tune to which he added a verse about a character called 'Eleanor Rigby'. This drew on memories of visits to provide company for solitary old people as a Boy Scout. He had never written before about a named third person, and lost on how to proceed, he sought advice. Several accounts refer to John, George and Ringo as well as Beatles' gopher, Mal Evans, and John's friend, Pete Shotton, adding ideas for the next two verses and the chorus. Capitalising on the confusion over who wrote what, in his long interview for Playboy magazine in 1980 John said: "the first verse was by Paul and the rest by me", to which Paul acidly replied that his partner's input was only "half a line". On reflection, the more surreal lines appear truer of John. The act of penning a sermon that will not be heard reads as a sardonic commentary on the lyrics Paul had written so far. Beyond this, knowing of his preference for writing about himself, it is hard to believe that John would have been interested in any of the characters and he was simply jealous of the success Paul achieved with the song.

Adding to the confusion on where the words came from was the revelation that there are graves with the names of 'Eleanor Rigby' and 'Father Mackenzie' in the grounds of St Peter's Church, Woolton, Liverpool – the very place John and Paul first met at a village fete in 1957. Paul, normally quite definite about what he did or didn't write, admitted to being bewildered by the news. The lyrics, it would appear, had a ghostly life of their own. There was no such ambiguity about the music. George Martin's score of strings for Paul's piano arrangement magnifies the emotions and was inspired by Bernard Hermann's film score for the thriller, *Fahrenheit 451*. While Hermann used taut, slashing strings to conjure up wide-eyed terror, here they suggest the bleakness of lives which end un-mourned; the polar opposite of the glow of love of the Lennon/McCartney songbook to this point.

THE END

Words: McCartney   Music: McCartney/ Lennon/ Harrison
Paul "Why don't we return to live shows?" John "I think you're crazy. I didn't want to tell you before, but I'm leaving the band" – conversation at Apple offices, September 1969.
It was John's idea for the three guitar contest. The guitar solos were recorded live in a single take. Paul's guitar is heard first, George's second and John's third.
The basic track including guitar solos was recorded on 23rd July with overdubs largely for vocals and strings on 5th, 7th, 8th, 15th, 18th August 1969
Found on *Abbey Road*

Paul was keen to get the Beatles to return to the stage and it is probable he envisaged 'The End' as a conclusion to their live shows. His message that we receive love equal to the amount we give would have had a dramatic impact live. If they had toured in the fall of 1969, the prospect of three Beatles playing lead guitar would have been a tantalising one too.

The guitar contest was John's idea to fill an instrumental break, but it was George who responded best, conjuring up a solo that owes more to Eric Clapton than to his own unflashy style. The solos of Paul, George and John in turn reflect the late 60s' trend for musicians to show off their musical virtuosity in long instrumental passages. To their credit they show how it should be done, each offering a teasing snippet that leaves the listener wanting more and not less. Likewise, Ringo, who had a horror of ostentation, at first point-blank refused to play a solo, until he was persuaded that nothing over-blown was required. Indeed, his solo is brief and accords with the entrance of the competing guitars.

EVERY LITTLE THING

Music: McCartney   Lyrics: McCartney/Lennon
Recordings on 29th September 1964 were scrapped and a good take was made the next day
Found on *Beatles For Sale*

Made barely a week after a 25-date concert tour of the US which left John so exhausted his first wife recalled him spending days in bed recovering, this is the most wearied the Beatles sounded on record. Photos from the session show them in sedentary poses and as George Martin later observed they were 'war-weary' when making *Beatles For Sale*.

The track has a funereal pace and audibly short of breath, John sings of a blissful romance in a tone of resignation. This melancholy twist has its fans and musically there is a disjoint too; each time the word 'little' is sung, it is followed by a double crash of a booming tympani drum. Lyrically, it covered old ground. Where on 'And I Love Her' Paul refers to a love that cannot die, so does 'Every Little Thing' and where, on 'Things We said Today' Paul says he is lucky for this, the same is said here.

EVERYBODY'S GOT SOMETHING TO HIDE EXCEPT FOR ME AND MY MONKEY

Lennon
"Everybody has got something to hide, we just want to be ourselves",
John 1980
Rehearsed over the evening of 26th June 1968 at Abbey Road studios,
a basic track was made the following evening with overdubs on 1st
July and 23rd July
Found on *The Beatles* aka The White Album

"Where's your wife?" shouted journalists who first saw John and Yoko Ono together in public in June 1968 at the National Theatre in London. His split from Cynthia Lennon was suddenly public knowledge and the ensuing media coverage was hostile and hurtful, especially for someone used to a more cosy relationship with the British press. Ten days later he was recording a response. However, instead of an angry riposte, he contrasted the media's prudishness with his desire to be open about all areas of his life. 'Everybody's got something to hide except me' was the stance. This was all added to a ditty John composed in India, entitled 'Come On', after a common encouragement from the Maharishi.

For a band that was now supposed to be riven by pettiness and rows, they achieved an extraordinary chemistry in bringing these words to life. The exciting switch of time signatures and sound textures shows the liberty that comes from a set of lyrics that do not say very much.

EVERYBODY'S TRYING TO BE MY BABY

Written by Carl Perkins
George idolised Carl Perkins so much that pre-fame he once used
Carl Harrison as a stage name.
Recorded in one take on Sunday 18th October 1964
Found on *Beatles For Sale*

This was originally a popular three-chord Country and

Western song from the 1930s, which Carl Perkins adapted in the 1950s to tell a tale of the craziness of his overnight fame. The '19 women' knocking on Perkins' door was altered to a more Beatles-sized 50 here, but the bawdier verses with their references to 'squalling' and 'balling' were left out to protect their media image. Perkins presumably adapted his verses from his experiences following his first national hit 'Blue Suede Shoes' in 1956.

One of six recordings made under pressure on 18th October 1964, George gave a rousing vocal on the very first take while also not putting a note out of place on two guitar solos. His reward was for this performance to be made the finale to the album.

FIXING A HOLE
McCartney
A basic track was made at Regent Sound Studios, Tottenham Court Road, London on 9th February 1967 with overdubs at Abbey Road on 21st February.
Found on *Sgt. Pepper's Lonely Hearts Club Band*

Paul contradicted popular belief this was a drug song for 31 years, by saying it was inspired by DIY carried out at his dilapidated farm in Scotland. Only when his autobiography was published did he admit it was an analogy for the effects of marijuana. Strong hints had been there all along. To disorientate the listener he sings in a strung-out vocal, the guitar is set to extreme reverb and jazz-style drumming is paired with a classical instrument, a harpsichord. The counter-cultural ideas John aired on *Revolver* are referenced throughout. The plea to let one's mind wander is made on 'Tomorrow Never Knows'. Where 'Dr Robert' could be a wholesome family doctor or an illicit provider of drugs to the in-crowd, the ambiguity around DIY and recreational drugs is summed up in the play on the words 'wonder'/ 'wander'. Where 'Rain' questions our reactions to 'bad' weather, Paul suggests what is 'wrong' is actually 'right' and when John taunts those who cannot see his point of view on 'And Your Bird Can Sing', Paul mocks the 'silly' persons who try to meet him, but go about it the wrong way. The mocking of those that rush is also found on 'I'm Only Sleeping'.

FLYING

Lennon/Harrison/McCartney/Starr
A twenty minute jam cut down to 90 seconds.
Basic track recorded on 8th September 1967 with overdubs on 28th September.
Found on *Magical Mystery Tour*

Long hours and a methodological approach typified *Sgt. Pepper's*, so to follow that album with a night of random music must have come as a big release. While certainly not magnificent, this jam is true to its intention of recreating the loss of control of a drug trip. In the *Magical Mystery Tour* film it accompanies a dream sequence of a bus as it symbolically takes off into the clouds. The spaced-out blues progression has a heavily-treated sound on guitar, but who plays it, the mellotron and the few notes on what sounds like a clavioline, has never been clear.

THE FOOL ON THE HILL

McCartney
A person who introduced himself as Jesus Christ was once brought by Paul to a Beatles' recording session to amuse the rest of the band.
Basic track recorded on 25th September 1967 with overdubs on 26th, 27th September, 20th October.
Found on *Magical Mystery Tour*

The only thing close to a conventional arrangement on the *Magical Mystery Tour* was, ironically, this ode to a 'fool'. Temporarily in awe to anything that broke with tradition,

Paul was inspired by the tale of a monk who lived in a cave throughout most of WW2. But consciously or not he was also writing about himself; his morning walks to Primrose Hill, close to his home, offered a panoramic view of central London, which suggests the line about watching the world turning round. The line also chimes with the kaleidoscopic vision John writes of in 'Lucy in The Sky with Diamonds'. Overall the words imply optimism for the fool's vision but the music emphasises loneliness, which tells us he is unlikely to find acceptance. The melancholy mix of minor sevenths, sixths and minor chords is played on instruments associated with solo performers – harmonica and recorder.

FOR NO ONE

McCartney
John cited this as one of his favourite tracks by Paul
A basic track of piano and drums were recorded on 9th May 1966, the vocals on 16th May and the French horn solo on 19th May.
Found on *Revolver*

Where Lennon/McCartney once lured in fans with the words 'you' and 'me' in song titles, choruses and first lines, here, Paul, pointedly addresses this for 'no one'. Several years into his relationship with Jane Asher, he was finding it hard to remain upbeat on the subject of love and at one point here he even refers to it as 'dead'. The cause was a row they had on a skiing holiday in Switzerland, where he found himself miles from home with someone he temporarily could not stand. The anxieties over being ignored that first surfaced on 'You Won't See Me' reappear. He describes her going out while he stays in and generally taking her time away from him and not hurrying to return. The tears, which he says, she cries for no one, are a possible allusion to Asher's acting ability, a starkly vicious line if true.

The arrangement sums up this clipped severity. There are no comforting harmony vocals from John and George, while the French horn solo has minimal backing, as if the rest of the orchestra had not shown up. The clavichord*, too, is music from another century and the playing lacks emotion; the chords fall relentlessly downwards, an effect used on the recent UK No.1 'Go Now' by the Moody Blues, a similarly bleak tale of a doomed relationship.

*The clavichord dates from the 1500s and is a small keyboard contained inside a rectangular box. Its sound is similar to a harpsichord.

FOR YOU BLUE
Harrison
Recorded on 25th January 1969
Found on *Let It Be*

George had two smart remedies for the imploding of John and Paul's partnership during the *Let It Be* sessions. One was to introduce US keyboard player, Billy Preston, to give the band a fresh foil. The second was to get his bandmates to dumb down to record this three-chord blues. Paul has the faux naif piano riff – George asked studio engineer, Glyn Johns, to capture a 'bad honky-tonk piano' sound, while John plays an equally simple but effective slide guitar accompaniment. In a rare moment of harmony both are captured on film grinning at this simplicity.

George appears to have reasoned the bad atmosphere on the sessions meant the simpler the song the more likely it was to shine. Indeed, this was the first *Let It Be* track to be completed satisfactorily after three weeks of meandering rehearsals.

While Elmore James, nicknamed 'the king of slide guitar', gets a name check here, 'For You Blue' owes more to Bob Dylan's 'Country Pie', a ramshackle blues which George would have heard when he visited Dylan in Woodstock, New York in late 1968.

FREE AS A BIRD
Words: Lennon/McCartney   Music: Lennon/McCartney/
Harrison/Starkey
REAL LOVE
Words Lennon Music Lennon/McCartney/ Harrison/Starkey
Found on *Anthology*
First released 1995-96

'Free as a Bird' began as a few verses that John recorded at home on piano in New York during his years out of the music business. A musing on his lack of commitments, it was a theme he would return to with more humour on 'Watching the Wheels'. 14 years after his death, the world's curiosity for a Beatles' reunion led the cassette to be eq'd, compressed and stretched to provide the remaining group with a steady tempo on which to play. George's neat slide guitar and Paul's mournful lyrics are handsome additions to John's sketch but ultimately guesswork on what he might have envisaged, while his voice is stretched so far it is stripped of personality.

By contrast, the overdubs to the up-tempo 'Real Love', another sketch recorded on cassette in New York, are more successful at suspending disbelief. George's tasteful answering phrases hold the momentum through all its verse and chorus changes.

FROM ME TO YOU
Lennon/McCartney
Single released 11th April 1963
At 1.56 seconds this is the Beatles' shortest single
It was a local hit in Los Angeles (reaching No.32), six months before the group became nationally famous in the USA.
Recorded in 13 takes on 6th March 1963
Found on *Past Masters*

All of the Beatles' singles were commercially calculated, but none as much as 'From Me To You'. After once being concerned at how their recordings would go down with their hard-core fans who saw them live in Liverpool, John and Paul now switched affections to teenage record buyers, who, to their delight, were sending them letters from across the country. Paul later explained, "We knew that if we wrote a song called 'Thank You Girl' that a lot of the girls who wrote us fan letters would take it as a genuine thank you... 'From Me To You' is another." A banal promise of fidelity, the lyrics offer a true heart, arms to hold them and lips to kiss, an age-old ploy among songwriters marketing pretty boy bands or singers.

Such naked ambition was encouraged by the success of fellow Liverpudlians, Gerry and the Pacemakers, who had gratefully received 'How Do You Do It?' after the Beatles rejected it and became the first Merseyside group to reach No. 1 in April 1963. Whilst remaining friends with Gerry Marsden the Beatles were piqued by this coup. Not that they needed much encouragement to follow in his footsteps; in February John quipped to London's Evening Standard newspaper: "We all want to get rich so we can retire".

How much of the commercial nous shown on 'From Me To You' was the Beatles' is debatable. Brian Epstein had made them smarten their appearances and even bow to acknowledge applause on stage. Also, in January they had signed an agreement to let Dick James act as their publisher. Though they later bitterly regretted this deal, it is probable he passed on commercial advice, as he had experience as a singer and song-writer.

EMI gave a short deadline to produce a single that would capitalise on the success of 'Please Please Me', so 'From Me To You' was pieced together on a coach journey from Shrewsbury to York on 28th February. Five days later it was recorded on a precious free day in their tour schedule. It is sparsely-arranged compared to the hook-laden 'Please Please Me', but its strength is an infectious enthusiasm that belies the venal lyrics. Extra appeal was boosted by George Martin's decision to place a chorus, which is faster than the opening verse, at the start to grab the radio listener's attention. 'From Me To You' duly spent an amazing seven weeks at No. 1 in the UK charts and by the summer fan hysteria was rapidly growing. Success came at a price. As Ringo later admitted, they found their return visits to Liverpool an embarrassment. Although their performances were a blast of energy compared to the pop scene of this era, their fans and friends back home were well aware of how much they had toned down their act.

> "We weren't as open and as truthful when we didn't have the power to be. We had to take it easy. We had to shorten our hair to leave Liverpool and get jobs in London. We had to wear suits to get on TV. We had to compromise. We had to get hooked, as well, to get in and then sort of get a bit of power and say, 'This is what we're like.' We had to falsify a bit, even if we didn't realize it at the time." *John Lennon*, Look Magazine, *December 1966*

GET BACK
McCartney/Lennon
Single released 11th April 1969, album version released 1970.
Recorded 28th January 1969
Found on *Past Masters* and *Let It Be*

The Beatles openly discussed splitting after a week of cold, tetchy, and aimless rehearsals in early January 1969. What saved them was a musical jam they stumbled into that reminded them of their very best work.

Starting from a bass line, all four of them plus maestro Hammond organ player, Billy Preston, fleshed it out over numerous daily run-throughs.

Whilst it took shape, Paul improvised absurd phrases in place of finished lyrics. Uncomfortably for posterity, he satirised the media furore around recent immigration, with the lines 'don't dig no Pakistanis taking all the people's jobs', sung in a foreign accent with a chorus line repeating the words 'get back'. As the days passed Paul replaced this with jokes about sex, drugs and Apple insider Chris (Christine) O'Dell who had moved from Tuscon Arizona to California and then London, to humour his sullen band mates. The fun lyrics, the infectious rhythm and the stake all band members had in the number brought focus. On the final run through they display a telepathy not heard since they were playing at the Cavern. The lean, dextrous musicianship allows several instruments a chance to shine and given time to rehearse, John felt comfortable enough to take on a rare virtuoso role, an opportunity seized after George's walkout in mid-January. He plays the taut Chuck Berry riff and the dreamy guitar solo which provides a release for the insistent, pent-up rhythm from a high bass line and skipping beat. This rhythm has its origins in 'Going up the Country' by Canned Heat, a chart hit of the time. Out-takes from the *Let It Be* sessions reveal the Beatles playing a snatch of the US group's hit. Its lyrics, too, are a tale of getting back to nature.

Two versions of 'Get Back' were created. The single is a straight studio performance, while the album version uses this take with added crowd noises, to give the impression of being live. The single also has a false ending where John leads the band back with a tougher attack on the Chuck Berry riff, a part actually edited from a separate performance.

GETTING BETTER
Music: McCartney   Words: McCartney/Lennon
"We shared a lot of feelings about teachers who had punished you too much", Paul '98
The basic track was recorded on 9th March 1967 with overdubs on 10th, 13th, 21st, 23rd March.
Found on *Sgt.Pepper's Lonely Hearts Club Band*

Initially nervous at how *Sgt Pepper's* would be received the group invited friends to hear early playbacks. Awed reactions were standard and it was all the confirmation they needed that their music was 'getting better' with every step. For Paul, this was gratifying, but it also sparked vengeful thoughts on his treatment as a schoolboy. So here he faced down the teachers who failed to spot his genius*, while the journalists who questioned whether the Beatles were finished, after a long silence following *Revolver*, could not have been far from his mind too. If Paul's vision was a little big-headed then John's glib asides 'I can't complain' and 'it can't get no worse' are a counterpoint. And if he was too light-hearted, then John's shameful admittance of violence towards his wife is a jarring, powerful contrast.

Underneath these exchanges was one of the richest musical tapestries ever captured on four-track recording equipment. To overcome its restrictions a solution was dreamed up to queue up each instrument for a solo on one of the four recording channels so as not to lose sound quality. In this way, the staccato rhythm guitar, lead guitar, drums, vocals and tambora (a stringed Indian instrument) are given a few seconds of tape to stand out, each with a uniquely enhanced sound. An orchestra will similarly allow instruments of varying pitch and timbre to shine and no other song better illustrates the pay-off for the long hours spent perfecting *Sgt. Pepper's*. Paul's lead vocals add to its texture with their rhythmic emphasis on the prevalent 'ter' sound in the title phrase. Surprisingly, all this complexity hides a simple F, C, G chord pattern.

---

*The counter-culture's criticism of the teaching they received at school is found on the Mothers of Invention album *Freak Out*. One of the first wilfully strange rock albums, its release in 1966 led Paul to proclaim *Sgt. Pepper's* would be the Beatles' own *Freak Out*. The opening track 'Hungry Freaks Daddy' castigates American schools 'who do not teach' and minds that won't be 'reached'.

GIRL

Lennon/McCartney
The only one word chorus on a Lennon/McCartney song. The
brevity was very likely due to the speed with which it was completed
on the last day of recording *Rubber Soul*.
Recording started and completed in the evening of 11th November
1965
Found on *Rubber Soul*

Three years into his marriage, John was beginning to recoil
from domestication and started to visualise the ideal
partner to escape with, going so far as to bring this person
to life in a lyric. The first verses are beguiling in their
picture of the cool girl who is strong enough to put him
down and with whom he is besotted, but there is a twist.
In the last verse the girl is a passive bystander while her
man works himself to death. To John it was an attack on
the protestant work-ethic, but it makes more sense as
Paul's old-fashioned view of Jane Asher pursuing a career
that took her away from him, while he was 'breaking his
back' completing *Rubber Soul* to deadline. Both claimed
credit for this verse and both worked on the music too.
John said 'Girl' was his first composition to match the
mood of its music to the lyrics. Indeed, the use of an East
European folk melody tells us the girl he wanted to meet
is either foreign or bohemian. Paul was familiar with
Russian and Ukrainian folk tunes through an interest in
New York folk duo, Gene & Francesca. He adapted one
of their songs 'Those Were the Days My Friend', for a
chart-topping single for Mary Hopkins in 1968. Both the
mood and melody of 'Girl' and 'Those Were the Days My
Friend' have a fatalistic air and the same lilting switch
between minor and seventh chords in the verse, before
moving to major chords in the chorus. John, in his way,
may have been looking to emulate Paul's 'Michelle' with
its slow tempo, same key, one word title and European
folk style.

GLASS ONION

Music: Lennon   Lyrics: Lennon/McCartney
The basic track was recorded on 11th September 1968 with overdubs on 12th, 13th September and 10th October.
Found on *The Beatles* aka the White Album

The rudimentary drum beat before John launches into 'Glass Onion' showed how far he wanted to move from the fancy production of *Sgt. Pepper's*. Its bluntness, too, displays the irritated mood with which he approached this task. John felt misrepresented by Paul's concept album and announced to staff at Abbey Road on the first day of *The White Album* sessions that he did not want to record any more 'rubbish' like it.

Its sarcasm was aimed at those who over-analysed the lyrics printed on the *Sgt. Pepper's* sleeve. Notably some had come to interpret Henry, the dancing horse on 'Being For The Benefit Of Mr Kite', as a code for heroin and 'When I'm 64' as a critique of retirement in a capitalist system.

The first version of 'Glass Onion', now on *Anthology 3* is truest to this intention. Its disembodied voices and sound effects are edgier than the strings which replaced them on the final version at George Martin's suggestion.

GOLDEN SLUMBERS/ CARRY THAT WEIGHT

Music: McCartney   Words: McCartney/ Dekker
The words were adapted from Thomas Dekker's song 'Golden Slumbers' written as part of *the Pleasant Comedy of Old Fortunatus* from 1599.
'Carry That Weight' was previewed as a solo song by Ringo on the *Let it Be* sessions. Notably here, his chorus vocal is pushed highest in the mix.
A basic track of Paul on piano, George on bass and Ringo on drums was made on 2nd July 1969. Overdubs were added on 3rd, 4th, 30th July, 15th August.
Found on *Abbey Road*

One of the most touching songs in the whole of the Beatles' oeuvre, the words tell of Paul's acceptance that his efforts to renew the band have failed and that this will haunt him for ever after. As his opening line acknowledges there is no way to 'get back' home, an allusion to his efforts to reignite the band's spark during their disastrous sessions in January. These emotions are expressed without his band-mates for the first 30 seconds with a delicate, mournful piano line, bass and weeping strings.

Heartbreakingly, Paul's solace is in being sung to sleep like a child, conjuring up a remembrance of his mother's love. Her absence was evoked while visiting his father in Liverpool. The lullaby lyrics for 'Golden Slumbers' were taken from a book of Elizabethan songs he found there. As he could not read notation he created his own tune. Where 'Golden Slumbers' shows his private sorrow, 'Carry That Weight' forces the whole band to face the consequences of their demise, by getting all of them to sing the chorus.

GOOD DAY SUNSHINE
Music: McCartney Words: McCartney/Lennon
"Me trying to write something similar to 'Daydream'", Paul '98
Basic track recorded on 8th June 1966 with overdubs on 9th June
Found on *Revolver*

This hymn to being commitment-free sums up Paul's lifestyle from January to April 1966, where, with no recording, concerts or TV appearances he was enjoying a new-found lack of responsibility. It picks up on the theme of a Chuck Berry's B-side 'Vacation Time', which tells of relaxing with his girlfriend on a sunny day under a 'shady tree', a phrase also used here. And it references 'Daydream' by the Lovin' Spoonful, which was in the charts in early 1966 and describes a sunny day spent lying on the grass. If 'Daydream' is an American hippie ode to getting stoned,

Paul's musical send up was to imagine an old-fashioned, upper-class Englishman singing. This stylisation is echoed in the stiff piano lines while the walking bass line mimics a dignified stroll in the park. If further proof were needed that this is a spoof, George Martin plays the honky-tonk piano solo – a role he repeated on Paul's other joke songs 'Lovely Rita' and 'Rocky Racoon'.

At the close, the sudden shift into phased psychedelic vocals, achieved through a delay on automatic double-tracking, is Paul stepping out of the joke, back into the hip world of the London in-crowd he was getting to know.

GOOD MORNING GOOD MORNING
Lennon
The cockerel that starts the song is the emblem of Kellogg's Corn Flakes, from whose advert John based the song's chorus.
Basic track recorded 8th February 1967 with overdubs on 16th February, 13th, 28th, 29th March
Found on *Sgt. Pepper's Lonely Hearts Club Band*

To produce material for an album with the highest standards was often a struggle. The first line here conjures up John's ennui at the growing regularity of his commute to and from Abbey Road studios in winter often in the middle of the night. The journey from his house in Weybridge, Surrey, to North London is approximately 75 miles as the crow flies. *Sgt. Pepper's* had clocked up close to 30 days work, but was only half-completed by the time 'Good Morning, Good Morning' was started.

John looked back with disdain, labelling the song as 'garbage'. Some see his reference to having 'nothing' to talk about as summing up the stupefaction of his home life, but it is more likely to refer to his perceived failure to bring any purpose to the words. He may have also come to be embarrassed at following Paul and coming up short. Its tale of a wander past his old school, the shops and coming back home for TV is not far off the tales of street life in 'Penny Lane'.

A frantic beat rushes the words with John's complaint of feeling low-down contrasted with machine gun-like drum-fills and Paul's waspish guitar solo. The conclusion with animal noises is similarly illogical. However, the chicken clucking at the end fitted neatly into the pitch of the guitar that starts 'Sgt Peppers Lonely Hearts Club Band (reprise)', achieving, as George Martin remembered, an edit luckier than he could ever have hoped for.

GOODNIGHT
Words: Lennon Music: Lennon/ George Martin
Recordings made on 28th June 1968 and 2nd July were scrapped to make way for a final take on 22nd July.
'Put all those toys away. Yes, Daddy will sing a song for you,' words at the start of an early take.
Found on *The Beatles* aka The White Album

Julian Lennon spent his fifth birthday without his parents who had taken a two-month trip to India to seek enlightenment. Guilt over this absence is then the likely reason for this sweet lullaby. John had further cause for guilt as soon after returning, he moved out to live with Yoko Ono. If forgiveness was the motivation, then it falls short. By passing the song to Ringo it lacks the honesty of 'Beautiful Boy', which he sang sweetly for his second son twelve years later. John had previously passed material he was too embarrassed to sing to Ringo, but on an album where he would shock fans many times over, it was perhaps asking too much for him to break another taboo, namely of a tough-talking rock star singing to his five-year old son. Paul, who heard the demo version, said that John sang it beautifully. Apparently an acetate disc of this performance was given to Ringo, though this is believed lost.

'Goodnight' is notable for displaying John's fascination

with dreams in his request to Julian to dream for him too. Sympathetically, George Martin gives a cinematic score that suggests the orchestration for a fantastical cartoon. Other than Ringo, who renders what he later described as a nervous vocal, no other Beatle was involved. On an album that is largely a hotch-potch of unrelated tracks, the sync-ing of 'Revolution No 9' and 'Goodnight' is a master-stroke. The soft, treacly violins and choir are like an idyllic dream after a long nightmare.

GOT TO GET YOU INTO MY LIFE

McCartney
"The mikes were right down in the bells of the instrument and then we limited the sound to hell. Prior to this people always miked brass something like six feet away." Geoff Emerick, chief engineer.
The first recordings on 7th April 1966 were scrapped, before a basic track was made on 8th April, with guitar added on 11th April and vocals and brass on 18th May
Found on *Revolver*

This not only emulates the Motown records Paul loved but takes them on a flight of fantasy long before the Detroit label acknowledged Psychedelia*. Continuing the anything goes themes of other *Revolver* tracks, this was, in Paul's words, an "ode to pot" masquerading as a love song. Musically brave, it took advantage of new sound limiters which allowed microphones to be placed directly into the apertures of the brass instruments giving enormous attack and presence. If the trumpets here were not true of Motown, which favoured saxophones, the metronome beat of a snare drum synchronised with the tambourine is. The trick is found on Stevie Wonder's 'Uptight' and the Supremes' 'Love Is Like An Itching In My Heart', both in the charts at the time of recording. *Only with the Supremes' single 'Reflections', with its science-fiction oscillator sounds, did this change.

HAPPINESS IS A WARM GUN

Lennon

George and Paul rated this their favourite *White Album* track
"One of my best, it's a beautiful song." John
Recordings on 23rd September 1968 were superseded by two good
takes on 24th September which were edited together. Overdubs were
added on 25th September
Found on *The Beatles* aka The White Album

The part of 'Happiness is a Warm Gun' which everyone
remembers is the doo-wop pro-gun satire, but its most
profound lyric is often overlooked – a public admission by
a Beatle of heroin use, at 0.59. John's admission is placed as
a scrambled image amongst several peculiar lyrical sections
and was written as John's relationship with Yoko became
obsessive. Written in sections; the first most surreal verse
was jotted down with Beatles' publicist, Derek Taylor, in
April 1968 on a night both got high and talked until the
early hours. Taylor reeled off random anecdotes from
which John selected images. Harry Nilsson's 'Without
Her', was on the turntable for the whole time and the scat
singing from it, 'do-do-do-dooo', is mimicked here. The
second section was written in May as Yoko entered John's
life, while in June, John wrote the anthemic finale after
seeing the words 'happiness is a warm gun in your hand' as
a headline or advert in *American Rifleman* magazine – he
recalled it as a "fantastic, insane thing to say". The magazine
was, and is, a mouthpiece for the National Rifle
Association, an organisation set up to protect the second
amendment of the USA, which gives Americans the right
to own guns. The phrase was especially sensitive as the
Vietnam War reached its height, and following the
assassinations of US political figures Martin Luther King
and Robert Kennedy and the wounding of the artist Andy
Warhol. This satire is all the more prickly for being played
as a mock-innocent 1950s' four-chord doo-wop. Always
wary of being taken too seriously, John's instinct was to

lace his social comment with a joke — at one point the word 'gun' is overlaid with the word 'woman'. This design is not entirely original: Frank Zappa and The Mother Of Invention's 'What's the Ugliest Part of Your Body?' on *We're Only In It For The Money*, released in January 1968, had used the same doo-wop style to make a mocking social message.

The many layers of 'Happiness Is a Warm Gun' captivated all four Beatles enough to deliver one of the best live group performances on the *White Album*. Its mix of five parts, each with its own tempo, required patience, as 70 takes and 24 hours of studio time were needed to record and mix it over three nights.

Freddie and John

'Happiness Is a Warm Gun' bears several similarities to Queen's 'Bohemian Rhapsody'. Neither has a chorus. Both hide references to dark secrets. Where John refers to his heroin use ('a fix'), Freddie Mercury appears to allude to his battles with coming to terms with his homosexuality. Both mix sex with violence, both refer to mothers, the use of the word 'trigger' is almost identical, as is the seemingly illogical mix of time signatures and moods.

A HARD DAY'S NIGHT

Lennon

The opening chord had long baffled guitarists until a mathematics professor from Dalhousie University in Canada used a computer to work out that the chord is backed with the note F played on piano to create a string of notes unplayable on one guitar alone.

"(The title is) a Ringoism. He didn't mean it to be funny, he just said it" John '80.

Recorded in nine takes on 16th April 1964

Found on *A Hard Day's Night*

Whereas professional song-writers were hired for the films

of Elvis Presley and Cliff Richard, John and Paul were protective of their image and so took on this role as well as acting. Their heavy workload inspired Ringo's quip "that was a hard day's night", which encouraged John to go home one night mid-filming and bring it to life as a lyric. His words make for a believable account of someone who is glad to have finished a long day's work – one dreads to imagine a hired writer forced to empathise and bring it to life.

The rush to record three days after writing meant its structure was limited. Beyond the strong opening lines and middle eight John had no time to expand and he ends up repeating the first verse three times. He also relied on 'Can't Buy Me Love's formula of a bluesy three-chord verse rooted in C, F and G, contrasted with an E minor, A minor laden middle eight.

The Beatles' creative control was not total: the arrangement was speeded up so much their complaint sounds happy. George Martin had been instructed by the film's producers to match it to the footage of fans chasing the Beatles into Marylebone train station, while the stark, suspended G chord on 12-string guitar was intended to announce the film's start in the manner of a morning reveille. The speeding up explains why it is Paul who had to sing the minor chord refrain ('when I'm home..') whilst John might have hit these high notes at a slower speed, once speeded up he was struggling. This is a happy accident, as Paul's vocal gives a welcome contrast to the repetition of John's verses.

A HARD DAY'S NIGHT (Album)

Recorded in 36 hours, mixed in 22 hours.

A Hard Day's Night contains only 13 tracks compared to the usual 14 for a Beatles' album. Another was planned, but Ringo fell ill at the last recording session before a world tour. This caused it to be the shortest Beatles' album at 30 minutes and 59 seconds.

Album released 10th July 1964

This relentlessly happy album caught four young musicians in a state of ecstasy after a wildly successful trip to the USA. For John, the acclaim was an adrenalin shot so large he wrote prolifically – 'If I Fell' and 'I'm Happy Just To Dance With You' are written on the same piece of paper – singing lead on nine of the album's thirteen songs, to Paul's three and George's one. His euphoria meant even accounts of heartbreak sounded happy. By contrast, Paul responded with caution. Whilst aiding John's speedy output, he took months over compositions which aspire to rise above teenage pop. There was a protest to finding himself in the lap of luxury on 'Can't Buy Me Love', plus cautionary and mature tales of love on 'Things We Said Today' and 'And I Love Her'. The contrast can be seen in the cover photos. Where John looks at the camera proudly, head on, Paul is evasive or guarded.

Now using four-track recording equipment, tricky guitar parts and vocals were perfected at leisure on track four. The separation made the vocal harmonies all the more exciting and gave more clarity to lead guitar.

HELLO GOODBYE

McCartney
"A song about everything and nothing." Paul '67.
Single released 24th November 1967
Basic track recorded 2nd October 1967 with overdubs on 19th, 20th, 25th October and 2nd November.
Found on *Magical Mystery Tour*

A chart-topper so little talked of it is often overlooked. Rarely covered or cited as a favourite, it did not capture the zeitgeist in the way other Lennon/McCartney tunes did. If John were around today, he might say 'told you so' as he was unhappy that it was made an A-side rather than 'I Am The Walrus'. Bitterly, he damned Paul's song as 'crap' – at a time when many artists were taking rock into uncharted territory he felt his bolder approach should have received greater publicity.

In its defence, the Hawaiian finale to 'Hello Goodbye' is in the same vein of anything goes wackiness of the B-side. It is also three of the most highly-caffeinated minutes in the Beatles' oeuvre. Paul infectiously uses high notes to convey happiness and silences to convey sadness or negativity, all sung in a way as if he wanted the public to share the extraordinary fortune life had brought him. The positivity is as much in his high-pitched ecstatic sighs and moans as it is in the words. As he states, when someone says 'stop', he says 'start' and 'go'. An allusion to this is played out in the surprise ending where the music returns as a foot-stomping sing-along with the tom-toms high in the mix. Indeed, if at times the sentiment is in danger of getting overly anodyne, the cascading clatter of Ringo's drums saves it.

HELP!

Words: Lennon   Music: Lennon/McCartney
John rated this as one of his four best Beatles' songs.
"Very fat, very insecure and has completely lost himself." John remembering his mental state when writing 'Help!' in 1980.
Released as a single on 19th July 1965
Recorded in 12 takes on 13th April 1965
Found on *Help!*

John reacted to fame like a dissolute lottery winner, enjoying an excess of everything from women, to drugs, drink, food and shopping. His grand new suburban house notably left Bob Dylan scornful of the way it was filled with superfluous toys and luxuries after he came for a short visit. Growing chubby and isolated, often idly watching TV, John, too, began to realise this might not be what he wanted. His unease was worse for being contractually obliged to appear in a film he came to despise: a slapstick comedy given the light-hearted title 'Help!'. When Dick Lester, the director, requested a song of the same name, John took the connotations personally and wrote a soulful lament which the film in no way deserved.

Originally slowly strummed on acoustic guitar, commercial realities meant it could not stay like that. Pressure to speed it up came from George Martin, the group, and indirectly, the producers of the film. This transforms his woe into euphoria and makes John garble some words in an effort to cram them in. The only sympathetic note is Paul's ingenious and comforting counter-melody, sung a split second before John as if trying to cheer him up and coach him through his lines.

Bob Dylan had set a precedent for this soul-searching. Where on 'My Back Pages' the lyrics euphemistically (and a touch confusingly) refer to being 'younger' than in *the past*, John here reminisced on when he was 'younger' than *now*. So whereas Dylan looked back scornfully, by contrast John looked back wistfully on his youth as innocent and trouble-free.

The idea caught his imagination so much the chord pattern from 'My Back Pages' is his starting point too. Dylan's verses start in C major, then pass through two minor chords before ending each stanza with three quickly-shuffled major chords, the last of which is a return to C major. 'Help!' follows the same pattern in the key of G major. In John's defence, the arrangement is souped up to a more powerful and tuneful effect. Furthermore, Dylan was no stranger to filching chord sequences.

HELP! (Album)
Recorded in 43 hours, mixed in 17 hours.
Album released 23rd July 1965

A fifth album of upbeat love songs with simple messages

was as far as John and Paul could stand. Out of habit they kept writing them, but the financial necessity had gone. Once written in the backs of vans, coaches, rehearsal rooms, cellars, council houses and low-budget hotels, now Paul would be chauffeured out to John's mansion for writing sessions. Where they once joked of 'writing a swimming pool' in a bid to goad themselves on, now lyrics and tunes were occasionally composed by a pool and four of the most forgettable songs with the Lennon/McCartney moniker were the result; 'Its Only Love', 'That Means A Lot', 'Tell Me What You See' and 'If You've Got Troubles'. It is at such points that many show-business careers peter out. However, both John and Paul were sensitive to being outshone and enviously espied the transformation Bob Dylan made months earlier, when he dropped the strait-jacket of worthy folk and protest for introspection with a dash of surrealism. His new message could be summed up as 'free your mind before you change the world'. On *Help!* three songs tentatively followed suit. John was first off the block with 'You've Got to Hide Your Love Away' in February and then again with 'Help' in April. In June, Paul followed with the prettier and similarly honest 'Yesterday'.

If the other songs on the album did not reach such heights, there were other strategies afoot. Many feature a bitter-sweet contrast between happy music and dark lyrics. All were receiving greater time too, as touring schedules were trimmed. This allowed the luxury of a live recording of drums, bass and rhythm guitar over which vocals, lead guitar and piano would be overdubbed and perfected at leisure. This made the intricate 'Ticket to Ride' and 'Help' slicker, but gave a dead sound to 'The Night Before' and 'You Like Me Too Much'. The process brought greater scrutiny of each instrument. Norman Smith, chief engineer, recalled Paul being openly critical of George's playing on 'Another Girl' and 'Ticket to Ride'. While neither has openly commented on this, it was undoubtedly a source of resentment.

HELTER SKELTER
McCartney
"We decided to do the loudest, sweatiest rock number we could."
Paul '85
The first recordings on 18th July 1968 were scrapped and remade on 9th September with overdubs added the following day.
Found on *The Beatles* aka The White Album

A week before recording 'Helter Skelter', John flew into a rage with studio engineer, Geoff Emerick, over his inability to give him a distorted sound on his guitar. The Beatles had no aspirations to being a heavy metal group, but felt pressure to show they could tackle any new trend. Paul, in terms of his competitive relationship with John, wanted heavy guitar distortion too, and he cited a desire to go one level louder and wilder than The Who as his initial inspiration for 'Helter Skelter'. Paul was intrigued by a boast made by The Who's guitarist and song-writer, Pete Townsend, that he had made the loudest and most powerful single ever. 'I Can See For Miles' had been held back from release for five months after recording during which Townsend had teased anyone who would listen as to how its power would blow away his rivals on release. Yet Townsend's hype was greater than the record's impact which stalled at No. 10 in the UK charts and at No. 9 in the USA. Paul, too, was underwhelmed and took it upon himself to create the noise he had expected. To do this the guitars were tuned low, then distorted and backed with white noise, while, in Paul's words the drums were hiked up "loud and horrible". In this spirit of excess, a chemical high was sought, an unusual step for a group that usually separated drug-taking from recording. According to studio engineer, Brian Gibson, they were "completely out of their heads" and Paul's stifled sniggers suggest cocaine use, which explains their drive to play some takes for as long as 20 minutes. The ending of one of these marathon performances with Ringo's plaintive cry for it all to end, "I've got blisters on my fingers" was tagged onto a more regular three minute take.

That the song survived this freak out is due to its subtle construction: eerie chords on the intro, a modulating riff and words open to a fair amount of interpretation. Paul refers to the aim of outstripping 'I Can See For Miles', with his boast of being 'miles above' while the fairground helter-skelter slide is an allusion to cocaine: the feeling of anticipation at the top of the slide, the spiralling adrenalin rush of the ride down, with the only way of repeating the high being to climb back up. The reference to a 'lover' in the lyrics makes it clear the 'ride' is also sexual.

HER MAJESTY

McCartney
Paul decided to cut this from *Abbey Road*, but teenage engineer, John Kurlander, stuck it on the run-out tape for the album's final mix where it stayed.
Recorded in three takes on 2nd July 1969
Found on *Abbey Road*

On 'Penny Lane' Paul had rhymed the word 'queen' with a euphemism for a penis ('machine'). Here he went one further with a fantasy about seducing the Queen of England. Couched in playful terms, any offence was overlooked, though public reaction at home might have been different had it retained its original album-placing between a ditty about a dirty old man ('Mean Mr Mustard') and a woman with a fetish for polythene ('Polythene Pam'). Run together, the three songs evoke a drunken, bawdy night out in Liverpool.

'Her Majesty' was written as a reaction to the first TV

documentary about the British royal family to allow cameras into their private lives.

HERE COMES THE SUN
Harrison
The most popular Beatles' song on iTunes, it is also the most popular Beatles' song on YouTube for a single video, though 'Hey Jude' has a similar number of hits based over 10 separate videos.
"It seems as if winter in England goes on forever; by the time spring comes you really deserve it." George '80
A basic track of George on acoustic guitar, Paul on bass and Ringo on drums was made on 7th July 1969 with overdubs on 8th 16th July, 6th, 15th and 19th August
Found on *Abbey Road*

Freak weather conditions in London at the start of 1969 saw February and March record the coldest start to spring for the whole of the 1960's. The situation was then reversed with April becoming the sunniest in the London region for 25 years* and the four-day Easter break going down as the brightest on record. On one of these warm days in April George walked out into the garden of his friend, Eric Clapton, guitar in hand, and created a song to match his joy. The light, delicate notes evoke the first wispy sun rays of morning, of bird-song and the opening of flower buds. Indeed, the sight of nature springing back to life must have been an adrenalin surge for someone who made gardening his pastime in his later years.

There were other reasons for rapture. George had slunk off to Eric's house to stay out of phone contact with his band-mates so as to avoid one of a string of business meetings arranged to sort out their new management and the problems of their Apple enterprise. As he recalled, "the relief of not having to go and see all those dopey accountants was wonderful". George had also endured a miserable winter, he had rowed with his band-mates on the *Let It Be* sessions in January, he had temporarily lost his singing voice to tonsillitis in mid-February and the threat of prison had hung over his head in March, when he was busted for possession of marijuana. 'Here Comes the Sun' was created soon after his case was discharged. As such, it does not just represent a relief that spring has come, but heralds the end of a crisis. As on 'Something' George managed to tap into a universal emotion that ranks as one of the greatest affirmations of life in popular music.

Such affirmations were in vogue in early 1969. The musical *Hair* which the Beatles individually attended, uses the sun as a symbol of optimism and enlightenment for a whole generation with 'Good Morning Starshine' and 'Let the Sunshine In', while the beginning of a new age is likened to sunrise on 'Aquarius'.

* The winter of 1962/63 is remembered as one of the coldest of the century in Britain, but the start to 1969 is notable for its contrasts. January 1969 was unremarkable, but February was particularly cold with the Met Office in Greenwich, London recording a minimum of -1c and a maximum of 4.9c. March was also colder than normal recording a minimum of 1.5c and a maximum of 7.7c. April was above average in temperature and saw an extraordinary 189 hours of sunshine, a record that stood from 1959 – when records began for the London area – to 1984.

HERE THERE AND EVERYWHERE

Music: McCartney Words: McCartney/Lennon
Written on a sunny day in June by the side of John's swimming pool
The first recordings on 14th June 1966 were not used. A good take was achieved on 16th June with overdubs added on 17th June.
Found on *Revolver*

In the same way 'Tomorrow Never Knows' reads like religious incantation, so does 'Here There And Everywhere', with its reference to seeking a 'better life'. Inspiration also came from the Beach Boys' 'God Only Knows' – a record Paul described at the time as 'the best ever made'. Both speak of an infinite love – Paul drawing inspiration from his three-year relationship with Jane Asher and to fit this purpose he pulled out of the drawer a special melody he had kept in reserve for over a year. In this God-inspired setting it was only natural to seek aural perfection and the Beatles duly gave a serene performance with feather-light instrumentation and celestial choir-boy vocals. Explaining his falsetto pitch, Paul claimed he sought to imitate the tone of Marianne Faithfull, though actually he sounds, logically, more like Carl Wilson's falsetto lead on 'God Only Knows'. He has commented since that this was the only time he could remember John openly praising him. John's admiration surely arose as the lyrics, which use each word of the title to start a different verse in turn, are as clever as the tune itself.

HEY BULLDOG

Lennon/McCartney
"A great sounding record that means nothing," John '80
Recorded in ten takes on 11th February 1968
Found on *Yellow Submarine*

One quirk of John's nonsense verse was the odd line with real meaning. The part sympathetic, part-taunting, offer of friendship on 'Hey Bulldog' is aimed at somebody, but there is no clarity as to whom. Some have suggested Paul, however, as John was close to the end of his marriage with Cynthia Lennon then she makes a likely target. It was created in the studio after the group was unable to sit still during the task of miming to 'Lady Madonna' for a promotional film. Always a fast worker, John arrived with a half-completed set of lyrics which he and Paul finished and then recorded in a single day. His energy was infectious; George quickly coming up with a fast and furious solo to match. Excited by its quick turn-around, John wondered aloud if this could make the next A-side instead of 'Lady Madonna'. George Martin settled the debate by saying it was too late to prepare for their scheduled release date.

The closing banter between John and Paul appears improvised, yet a similarly worded exchange appears at the end of Lonnie Donegan's 'Midnight Special' – a staple of their early live repertoire.

HEY JUDE
McCartney
The most successful Beatles' single, selling 7.5m copies in the four years after its release.
In its day the full six minutes and thirty seconds made it the longest ever single.
Recorded live in the studio at 2.55-2.59 someone (Paul, John or George) swears after hitting a wrong chord.
Saint Jude, one of the 12 apostles of Jesus Christ, is the patron saint of lost or hopeless causes.
First released as a single on 26th August 1968
Rehearsed at Abbey Road on 29th, 30th July 1968, the main performance was recorded at Trident Studios in Soho, London on 31st July with overdubs added on 1st August
Found on *Past Masters*

The gradual transformation from desolate mood to ecstatic is so subtle here it retains its fascination over repeated listening. While Paul has never fully acknowledged it, 'Hey Jude' was written as a form of catharsis in the wake of the sudden split from long-term girlfriend and fiancée, Jane Asher. As he tells it, it started as a ditty sung in his car while on his way to see John's ex-wife Cynthia and her son, Julian. Paul had built up a bond with Julian and he intended 'Hey Jules', as it was briefly called, to cheer up the five year-old, yet, the message echoed his own life too. Nine days before its recording, Jane had announced their engagement was over in a TV interview, after she found Paul in bed with another woman and the desolate opening

Hey Jude – **Returning the Compliment**

The Beatles were never shy of recognising the black artists that inspired them and the compliment was often quickly returned.

Jimi Hendrix acknowledged the imitation of himself on the title track to Sgt. Pepper's by making it a regular in his live set. Paul wrote 'Lady Madonna' in the style of Fats Domino and Fats duly covered it himself. 'The Long And Winding Road' was inspired by Ray Charles' 'Don't Let The Sun Catch You Crying' and Charles duly recorded Paul's pastiche. Less obvious is the connection between Wilson Pickett and 'Hey Jude'. Pickett made the Beatles' smash a hit for himself in 1968, yet the 'naaa, na-na-na, naaa, na-na-naaa' chant on his 1967 hit 'Land of 1000 Dances' is not a million miles from the chant on 'Hey Jude'. Oddly, the Wilson Pickett version of 'Hey Jude' succeeds largely with the chant buried deep in the mix.

verses ring powerfully true.

The recording saw the Beatles' love for the studio reawakened after a string of sonically lacklustre singles. It was their first to use eight recording channels – technology that brought a broader and cleaner sound than the four-track equipment they had used since 'I Want to Hold Your Hand'. Its possibilities excited Paul so much he teasingly introduced each of the tracks in turn. So the listener is treated to a trickle of new activity that evolves tantalisingly from lament to massed singalong. At first Paul is alone on vocals and piano, then tambourine, backing vocals, drums, bass and acoustic guitar are all added one by one. Nothing lifts the mood more than the point at which Paul's vocals are joined by his band-mates, John and George. Their vocals neatly introduce the triumphant three and a half minute orchestral coda – one of the most cathartic expressions of joy on record. While starting from nothing and building up to a big crescendo is a centuries old trick – Beethoven's Ninth Symphony with its 'Ode to Joy' choral section and Otis Redding's 'Try A Little

Tenderness' with its big brass ending are both good examples – few have done it better.

HOLD ME TIGHT
McCartney/Lennon
Such was this recording's faults that when the New Musical Express reviewed *With The Beatles* in November, the reporter wondered if his copy was warped.
A first recording on 11th February 1963 was rejected and was re-recorded in nine takes on 12th September
Found on *With The Beatles*

Best known for its out-of-tune vocals and wobbles in tempo, 'Hold Me Tight's lyrics, a series of stone age permutations around the words 'tight', 'tonight' and 'feeling right', have unjustly escaped ridicule. Written in 1961 when John and Paul were still songwriting novices, it owes its survival to its popularity at the Cavern and no doubt for the glee of putting an open reference to sex onto record. The faults in its performance, however, are due to tiredness. Out-takes reveal Paul struggling with his vocals. Even on the finished take, he wavers in and out of tune, finally breaking completely. Fatigue affects the group too, the tempo wavers and the guitars, which are double-tracked, have a dull, clumsy sound. Photos taken in Abbey Road studios on this day, show Paul and George looking drawn and spent. Clearly their heavy workload had caught up with them. 1963 was arguably their busiest year as they criss-crossed the UK on coaches between ballrooms, TV studios, press interviews and recording sessions. It is tempting to speculate that the night before the recording they had been celebrating too, as 'She Loves You' had just become No. 1 on all UK charts.

HONEY DON'T

Written by Carl Perkins
First released by Carl Perkins as the B-side to 'Blue Suede Shoes' in
early 1956.
Recorded in five takes on 26th October 1964
Found on *Beatles for Sale*

A BBC radio broadcast from 1963 captures John singing
'Honey Don't' with an earthiness and attitude missing
here. Ringo strains to bring any variation to the repetitive
lyrics; the sea-sick way he utters 'I'm feeling fine' mid-way
through is one of the most uncomfortable moments in the
whole of the Beatles' oeuvre. In fairness, he appears under-
rehearsed and his voice lacks the echo applied to the other
Carl Perkins cover 'Everybody's Trying To Be My Baby',
from these sessions. The group rarely turned out shoddy
work, but if it was one of Ringo's outings then it was more
readily accepted. To hear how it should be done, listen to
Perkins' original which is a revelation for the menacing
effect of echo on his vocal and for his powerful guitar
playing.

HONEY PIE

McCartney
John plays a rare and inspired guitar solo that Paul likened to the
playing of legendary jazz guitarist, Django Reinhardt.
Paul picked 'Cheek To Cheek' by Fred Astaire and the Hoagy
Carmichael song 'Stardust' in a list of his 10 favourite songs.
A basic track of Ringo on drums, George on bass, Paul on piano and
John on guitar was recorded on 1st October 1968 with overdubs on 2nd
and 4th October
Found on *The Beatles* aka The White Album

Paul has an early and enduring love of songs from the
1920s-30s, but this is so casual it has led many to label it a
humorous pastiche, despite his protestations it is not.
George Martin's replication of the sound of a dance band

makes the tune convincing, but it misses the input of John as lyric doctor to make it whole. When Paul rhymes 'crazy' with 'lazy' and sings it in the manner of an upper-class fop from a Hollywood film, it lacks the dry wit of Cole Porter whom he was aspiring to mimic. John was engaged enough to give a spirited jazz-inflected guitar solo, but he and Paul were by now hardly collaborating outside of the studio and it is word-play which was needed. That Paul understood its failure is clear by its placing as the only composition of his on *The White Album's* dreaded fourth side, which contained songs that were either controversial, ('Revolution 1' and 'Revolution 9'), or by general consensus weak ('Cry Baby Cry').

I'M A LOSER

Music: Lennon/McCartney   Words: Lennon
"(That was) pretty brave of John," Paul
"Attaining it was the big let-down. I found I was having continually to please the sort of people I'd always hated when I was a child."
John '80
Recorded in eight takes on 14th August 1964
Found on *Beatles For Sale*

Startling in its brutal self-loathing the opening lines of 'I'm A Loser' were written at the height of Beatlemania and ran counter to every expectation of how John should feel. For him a different side to success had become apparent after a tiring tour of Europe, Hong Kong, Australia and New Zealand. Being cooped up in hotels and aeroplanes, being expected to maintain a charming suit-and-tie image alongside the realisation this was not bringing all the riches it should after some poor business decisions* was demoralising. The very restrictions he was working under even led him to fudge his candid admission with an unconvincing resolution as a story about losing in love.

Inspiration was taken from Bob Dylan. The way the

listener is addressed as 'my friend' was used on 'Blowin' In The Wind'.

*The inexperience of Brian Epstein, the group's manager, led to millions being lost on merchandising and a paltry 7.5% of revenues from the film *A Hard Day's Night.*

I'M DOWN
McCartney
"I used to sing (Little Richard's) stuff but there came a point when I wanted one of my own." Paul '98
The B-side to 'Help!'
Recorded in seven takes on 14th June 1965
Found on *Past Masters*

A B-side of a vinyl single that parodies its A-side was the sort of elaborate joke the Beatles used to keep themselves sane during the height of Beatlemania. On 'Help!' John feels 'down' but here Paul feels 'upside-down', which as the flip-side of the single is exactly where he was. Such japes were perfect for the exercise of trying to mimic the manic singing of Little Richard and the power chord structure of his big hit 'Long Tall Sally'. This is not a complete Little Richard pastiche as the Beatles drew on a contemporary hit for inspiration too. 'Woolly Bully', by Sam the Sham and the Pharaohs, is the influence for John's wild Hammond organ playing. Meanwhile, the rough and ready guitar from George actually pre-empts its use on US punk and garage records such as 'Pushin Too Hard' by the Seeds and 'Dirty Water' by the Standells.

I AM HAPPY JUST TO DANCE WITH YOU
Lennon/McCartney
Paul described it simply as songwriting practice.
Recorded in four takes on 1st March 1964
Found on *A Hard Day's Night*

'I don't want to hear you say goodbye, I just want to dance until I fly'. Unused line from original handwritten lyric for 'I Am Happy Just To Dance With You'.

Famous for his searingly candid lyrics, John was no stranger to insincere Tin Pan Alley clichés either. Written to pander to George's fans, this teenage dance hall tale typecasts him as the junior Beatle. While 'I Want to Hold Your Hand' was still in the charts, he has to sing not only that he does not want to kiss the girl in question, but he does not want to hold her hand. George struggles with the vocals on what sounds a rushed recording and in the *A Hard Day's Night* film, John directs a sarcastic "well done" at him after the song is mimed. This cavalier approach extends to an extreme take on the syncopated guitars used by the Searchers on 'Sugar and Spice', a recent hit and a favourite of John's.

I'M LOOKING THROUGH YOU
McCartney
"Jane went off and I said, 'OK then. Leave. I'll find someone else.'" Paul.
Two attempts (24th October and 6th November) were scrapped before a satisfactory recording was made on 10th November 1965, with vocals added the following day.
Found on *Rubber Soul*

It took the writing of the magnanimous 'We Can Work It Out' for Paul's relationship with Jane Asher to survive this character assassination. His anger and sulking over her stint acting in a play in Bristol, led to a temporary split. Bewildered and hurt, for someone usually so assured he entered into some uncharacteristic soul-searching. So there was pleading ('You Won't See Me'), reasoning ('We Can Work It Out') and resentment ('I'm Looking Through You' and the last verse from 'Girl').

Getting Ringo, the least musical Beatle, to play the artless stabs of Hammond organ, whose overloaded sound pushed the recording limiters into the red, shows his venom, but the unkindest cut came in the harping over how their social standings had changed. Jane, he says, was once 'above' him, but he is now looking 'down' on her. The privately-educated and well-connected actress provided him with an entrée into social circles in London society, but, markedly, a week before recording the Beatles had achieved one of the ultimate symbols of class and status, a meeting with the Queen of England to receive an MBE medal during which jokes and casual chat were exchanged. Ad-libbing at the track's conclusion, he accuses Jane of being 'nowhere', a rebuke that must owe something to 'Nowhere Man' recorded only two days before. Ultimately, this flailing rage would subside, but the speed between writing and recording left it captured in amber.

I'M ONLY SLEEPING

Words: Lennon   Music: Lennon/McCartney
"How can you think if you are doing something all the time?…I'm not lazy. I've done more in ten years than most people would do in their life." John '80.
The Lovin' Spoonful's ode to sloth, 'Daydream', was a chart hit when 'I'm Only Sleeping' was being recorded.
The backing track was made on 27th April 1966 with overdubs on 29th April, 5th and 6th May.
Found on *Revolver*

In the first three months of 1966 John laid back in his home and divided his time between reading, thinking, getting high and sleeping. For someone with such an active imagination this was pure serenity, a state of well-being worth eulogising as much as love or peace. His description of drifting 'downstream', connects it to his explicit paean to LSD 'Tomorrow Never Knows', in which he had sung of floating 'upstream' – a possible allusion too, to the trip

Alice takes in *Through The Looking Glass*.

It caught the group's imagination too. The opening upstroke of guitar is like the flexing of outstretched arms or the pulling back of curtains to let the light in. The bass plods like a person getting out of bed only half asleep, while George's amazing backwards guitar solo with its yawning effect, took a six-hour session to work out so that it fitted the chords. John sings in the whiny voice of someone who has had their sleep disturbed, an effect achieved by vari-speeding his vocal, though it is not him who contributes the yawn – at 1.57 you can faintly hear John instruct 'Yawn Paul'.

'Watching The Wheels' from 1980 is a rewrite of this philosophy. Here his downtime, a five-year lay off from the record industry, is portrayed as a wise move and as an escape from the frivolity of the 'merry go-round', unlike 'I'm Only Sleeping' where he describes himself as 'wasting' time. On the 1980 track, his words are accompanied by a marvellously-echoed grand piano to emphasise the confidence of this view.

I'M SO TIRED

Lennon
Recorded in 14 takes on 8th October 1968
Found on *The Beatles* aka The White Album.

Suffering from insomnia whilst at meditation camp in India, John cheered himself up by writing a 50's style rock 'n' roll lullaby. A combination of jet lag, an absence of alcohol or drugs and the effects of meditation were the causes of his insomnia and as the lyrics suggest he still had broken sleep three weeks into his stay. The chords conjure up his growing weariness, with A major followed at each bar with a lower note, (e.g. 1st G#7, 2nd F#m7, 3rd E and finally Dm). Beautifully sung, John's stream of consciousness flows out in long sustained breaths. Paul was enamoured – an out-take exists of him attempting his own lead vocal too.

I AM THE WALRUS

Words: Lennon   Music: Lennon/ George Martin
"I was writing obscurely a la Dylan, never saying what you mean, but giving the impression of something, I thought well I can write that crap too". John '80.
B-side to 'Hello Goodbye'
Back track recorded 5th and 6th September 1967, brass strings and choir recorded 27th September.
Found on *Magical Mystery Tour*

In the group's first authorised biography John was portrayed as a drop-out from everyday life. Staring blankly into his garden or at the TV for hours on end, barely communicating, he appeared at a loss after the completion of *Sgt. Pepper's*. Biographer Hunter Davies, who visited him over the course of 1967, saw scraps of paper with single lines or verses strewn around the Lennon household, one of which formed the statement that 'I', 'you' and 'we' are all the same. His existence unmistakably tells of the ego death brought on by too much LSD and John's only complete composition from the second half of the year is merely a patchwork of these ideas. However, not all of his faculties were dulled, as this nonsensical structure served as a joke. Most commonly it is said to be aimed at a teacher from his secondary school who was now discussing his lyrics in class and was also a parody of Dylan's obtuse verse, though from conversations John had with Davies, it appears more of a swipe at the general public. John moaned about how the public read too much into his lyrics and his disconnected verse mirrors their misinterpretations. He said to Davies: "We know people want to be conned. They've given us the freedom to con them. Let's stick that in there, we say, that'll start them puzzling." In the midst of this morass John inserted a riddle giving a hint at this intent. His description of himself as 'the walrus' was taken from a poem in *Through the Looking the Glass* which depicted the walrus as an imperious conman. His other description of himself as the 'eggman' appears to refer to Humpty Dumpty, another character from the same book, who is shaped like an egg and claims to know and understand every poem ever written and says 'when I choose a word it means just what I choose it to mean'.

As slick as this conceit was in theory, John miscued. Unknown to him Lewis Carroll used the walrus to represent an avaricious capitalist – a finding that left him embarrassed.

The riddle is echoed in the music. The demented voices of the Mike Sammes Singers sing 'No' throughout as if confounding anyone's attempt at guessing what the words mean. Similarly, a heavy chord descent is matched with haphazardly ascending horns and strings. Recorded days after the death of the Beatles' manager, Brian Epstein, the group was temporarily in a state of shock and George Martin took on the bulk of the work, creating a fantastical array of harmonic interest to match the range of images in the words. Both Paul and George are barely noticeable and for such a big production to lack a starring role for Paul is exceptional. How much the mood concerned the loss of Epstein is open to speculation; the snatches of a radio adaptation from Shakespeare's King Lear, with its words ('Oh untimely death') are strangely prescient.

I CALL YOUR NAME
Lennon/McCartney
Dropped from the *A Hard Day's Night* film
Recorded in seven takes on 1st March 1964
Found on *Past Masters*

One of John's first attempts at songwriting at age 17 while

an art school student; a simple blues, the joy would have been in the creation, rather than any great meaning. He looked back fondly at this first step to his rewarding career and so once he and Paul had gained proficiency, they returned to restructure it with a middle eight and the ploy of a chord pattern that varies the second time it is played (e.g. E7, C#7, F#7, B7. E7, C#7, F#7, A). This was good enough to be handed to Brian Epstein's teenage protégée, Billy J. Kramer, who recorded a spirited version as the B-side to 'Bad to Me' in the summer of 1963. A year later it was remoulded with an instrumental break which lurches into ska tempo. The similarity of the ska rhythms to Millie's 'My Boy Lollipop' makes it probable John heard a pre-release in a London night club.

I DON'T WANT TO SPOIL THE PARTY
Music: Lennon/McCartney   Lyrics: Lennon
Recorded in 19 takes on 29th September 1964
Found on *Beatles For Sale*

Being invited to show business parties was a new perk for John in 1963-64, but amid the jollity he found it hard to let his competitive, side slip.

Cavern DJ, Bob Wooler, was left with broken ribs at Paul's 21st birthday party, when he mocked John for taking a holiday (a honeymoon as he put it) with Brian Epstein. A year later, British journalist and jazz singer George Melly retreated after sensing a boiling anger when he had lazily suggested the Beatles' music was all based on the blues. In a party at a New York hotel in 1964, John made a pass at Veronica Bennett of the Ronettes, which she politely declined. In her biography *Be My Baby* she recalled John slamming the door as he left. There are many more incidents from this era and pointedly John went as far as to describe 'I Don't Want to Spoil the Party' as "very personal". That he first offered it to Ringo, in a jaunty

Buck Owens style, suggests the emotions were not easy to confront.

I FEEL FINE
Music: Lennon/McCartney   Words: Lennon
Single first released 27th November 1964
Features the first ever use of feedback on a hit single
Recorded in nine takes on 18th October 1964
Found on *Past Masters*

John dragged his song-writing partnership with Paul from the brink of parody by providing a harder rock edge and an ambivalent take on the true-love theme of their earlier singles. The mention of 'diamond rings' so soon after 'Can't Buy Me Love' is surely not laziness but in fact irony – the love he sings of depends on materialistic favours, so it cannot be genuine. The message in the chorus is peculiarly half-hearted, the love for the girl in question is simply 'fine'. It could even be some sort of word-game as on the B-side Paul sings of his girl not needing any presents!

Bobby Parker's 'Watch Your Step'; a hit in the clubs, but too raw and overdriven to trouble the charts, is best known for providing the root of the guitar riff and its tale of a macho guy warning a girl about her behaviour is not far off the attitude John brings to his lyrics.

Impact was gained by double-tracking the riff. While George plays it first, a couple of bars in, John's guitar joins. The trick is heard on the riff used on Roy Orbison's 'Oh Pretty Woman', which was No.1 in the UK charts at the time. Though here, the tension is ratcheted up by adding an opening burst of feedback that was one part gimmick, one part one-upmanship on any pop group presumptuous enough to compete with them. On its release the Beatles coyly described the noise as an accident, but Mark Lewisohn's study of the original tapes (*The Beatles'*

Recording Sessions), reveals it was rehearsed over all nine takes.

I'VE GOT A FEELING
Music: McCartney   Lyrics: McCartney/Lennon
The *Let It Be* version was recorded live from the rooftop of the Apple headquarters in London on 30th January 1969. The *Let It Be Naked* version from 2003 is an edit of the two live performances of the song.
Found on *Let It Be*

This spoof of heavy feel-based rock could almost pass for the real thing. Yet Paul's 'oh yeah, oh yeah, oh yeah..Noooo!' exclamation shows his amusement at the style, which would morph into what is now known as heavy metal. The joke is shared with John who gleefully contributed an assortment of bizarre and mundane images. The irony of this try-out of free form rock was that Paul's precise instructions on what to play led to George storming out – an argument memorably captured in the *Let It Be* film. Happily, weeks later, this became one of the few songs on the album to fulfil its original premise of new material recorded live.

I'VE JUST SEEN A FACE
McCartney
"The lyric works: it keeps dragging you forward; it keeps pulling you to the next line, there is an insistent quality to it." Paul '98
Recorded in six takes on 14th June 1965
Found on *Help!*

This exuberant acoustic guitar workout's use of jazz, flamenco and Country and Western styles was an outlet for Paul's urge to stretch beyond a two electric guitar, bass and drums rock 'n' roll format. The sheer joy at this freedom is evident in his scat singing. The words are best understood in this context rather any literal meaning. Cited in his biography as one of his favourite songs it has remained in his live set to this day.

I ME MINE
Harrison
"I Me Mine is the ego problem." George, *Anthology*
Recorded in 16 takes on 3rd January 1970 with Billy Preston on organ, Paul on bass, George on acoustic guitar and Ringo on drums.
Found on *Let It Be*

George brought a passive-aggressive religious wrath down on John and Paul after his initial contribution to the *Let It Be* project, 'All Things Must Pass', failed to spark their interest. His message that to reach self-realisation one has to learn to live without thinking of a reward for each action, was a thought derived from the Bhagavad Gita, the holy text of the Hindu religion. Written in a single evening, after a day of frustrating rehearsals, George bluntly based its music from a BBC TV programme, *Europa-The Titled and the Untitled*, he was watching and presented it to the band the next day.

His anger was understandable. John and Paul lost interest with the pretty and delicate 'All Things Must Pass' after several passable run-throughs (one appears on *Anthology 3*), and suggested he record it solo on acoustic guitar. George felt the respect he showed to their compositions was not being returned. Whether they were conscious of the fact 'I Me Mine' was about them is not clear, but neither liked it; indeed John was recorded mocking the melody and like 'All Things Must Pass', George gave up on trying to perfect it during these sessions. Ironically, its rehearsals on 8th January 1969 were interwoven with performances of 'Let It Be' – another song which uses religious imagery as an outlet for grief caused by inter-band strife.

Owing to its inclusion in the *Let It Be* film, with

John and Yoko memorably dancing a waltz to it, a new version was made on 3rd January 1970 with a group made up of George, Paul, Ringo and Billy Preston (John being holed up in Denmark). Months later, Phil Spector added strings and repeated some sections, neither of which it merited.

I NEED YOU

Harrison/Lennon
Written about Patti Boyd, soon to be Patti Harrison.
"..the contributions I made to George's early songs like 'Taxman'. (I) never asked for anything or any recognition or anything from it."
John '80
Recording completed on 16th February 1965
Found on *Help!*

George revealed in a music paper interview from early 1966 how he and John had stayed up late one night putting the finishing touches to 'I Need You' and 'You Like Me Too Much'. John's input is likely to be the ploy of having the verses dominated by major chords to plainly lay out the facts of the story, then minor chords and harmony vocals to make a winning heartfelt plea on the middle eight.

This teamwork extended to the studio. George had acquired a guitar volume pedal – a sensitive device used to emphasise certain notes or chords. When it was too difficult to coordinate it was discarded and instead John knelt in front of George's guitar and turned its volume control for similar effect. The clipped chords of 'I Need You' suggests manual assistance, while the high-pitched whine on 'Yes It Is' suggests the use of a pedal.

I SAW HER STANDING THERE

McCartney/ Lennon
"We realised we were going to have to stop these bad lines or we were only going to write bad songs." Paul '98
Studio notes show this song was originally named as '17'
Recorded in nine takes on 11th February 1963
Found on *Please Please Me*

As a junior songwriter Paul here used a song he knew inside out – Chuck Berry's 'Little Queenie' – as a blueprint. Both are sung as if regaling a friend, with liberal use of the word 'well' as a device to show a change of tack. Both are tales of spying a beautiful 17 year-old at a dance. Berry sings of a girl 'standing' next to a jukebox (a 'record machine'), while Paul's girl is simply 'standing there'. Both share the next line which tells of the girl suddenly looking their way. And while Paul's girl is beyond comparison, Berry's is cute enough to appear on a magazine cover. The emotional impact gives Berry lumps in the throat and 'wiggles' in his knees, while for Paul it makes his heart go 'boom'. The similarities would be more obvious if John had not insisted on dropping the line 'never been a beauty queen'. The main difference is in the resolution. We never find out if Berry has his feelings reciprocated, whilst Paul wins the girl over.

On the other side of the world, in early 1963, Brian Wilson hit upon a similar idea of basing the Beach Boys' early hit, 'Surfin USA', on 'Sweet Little Sixteen'. Whilst Paul openly admitted to using Berry's riff from 'Talkin Bout You', 'Surfin USA' is for legal reasons now credited to Berry/Wilson.

I SHOULD HAVE KNOWN BETTER

Lennon
The Ska-talites played this song over and over again as an instrumental for the Jamaican Independence Day celebrations in 1964, while travelling round Kingston on the back of a lorry.

Recordings made on 25th February 1964 were scrapped and re-made in 18 takes on 26th February
Found on *A Hard Day's Night*

'Iiiiiiiiiiiiii'. John's long opening cry is one of the happiest in popular music. The lyrics may not have meant much, as he recalled, but the way it is sung does. Recorded after a triumphant first trip to the USA, the infectious tone reveals his feelings over success. The group had flown into New York apprehensive about how they would be received, but got a frenzied welcome. This was a tremendous boost for John, whose insecurities were never far from the surface. In this manner his shouts of 'hey-hey-hey' and his description of being happy inside and loving 'everything', make more sense as a paean to his amazing success.

This fever drives the pace but George's precise and thick-as-treacle chords on a 12-string Rickenbacker acquired in New York, act as a comforting and gorgeous anchor.

I WANNA BE YOUR MAN

McCartney/Lennon
"September 1963. No songs, at least none that we thought would make the charts... (John and Paul) gave us a song that was on their next album, but wasn't coming out as a single." Keith Richards, '10
Recorded in six takes on 12th September 1963 with overdubs on 3rd and 23rd October
Found on *With the Beatles*

Fame allowed John and Paul to develop a side-line in placing their weaker compositions with other artists and demand went through the roof after 'Bad to Me' by Billy J Kramer became their first giveaway to reach No.1 in September 1963. Hungry for the same success, that very month the Rolling Stones called in a favour from their new friends. After a chance meeting on a London street, the Stones 19 year old manager, Andrew Loog Oldham, persuaded John and Paul to turn up at the Stones' rehearsal room on Great Newport Street, where they knocked into shape a half-formed idea they had been toying with for over a year. Completed in minutes, it was crafted for the Stones' straight-ahead rock, a world away from minor chord-laden ballads such as 'Bad to Me'. Indeed, the stuttered way the chorus ends on the word 'man', is the same as on 'Fortune Teller', then in the Stones' repertoire, which ends on the word 'love'. The sight of such quick work was inspirational for the Stones who had not yet written a single song to their name. Their version became their first Top 20 hit in spite of a rough production. Its strengths were the sexual insinuation Mick Jagger brought to the words and a scorching slide guitar solo from Brian Jones. By contrast, Ringo never convinces and he is only saved by John and Paul sharing the chorus. Their added whoops and screams were included to encourage him into singing.

I WANT TO HOLD YOUR HAND

McCartney/Lennon
The first Beatles' track recorded on newly available four-track equipment gave greater clarity to harmony vocals, which could now be recorded on separate tracks.
Recorded in 17 takes on 17th October 1963
Found on *Past Masters*

To sing of loyalty and playground intimacy was an incredible act of focus from two young men who were well on the way to becoming the most sexually-promiscuous in a not yet swinging London. Its lines of endearment as if sung by fairy-tale minstrels, were knocked together in a few hours between gigs, in the small stuffy basement music room at Jane Asher's house at 57 Wimpole Street. Both

John and Paul appear to be writing sections in turn, leading to its thrilling structure that makes it hard for the listener to guess where the next chord or lyric was coming from. The twin vision is evident in the role given to Paul's harmony over John's lead vocals. On the words 'hide' at the end of the verse and 'hand' at the end of the chorus, Paul sings a humorous falsetto, a knowing ploy that drove live audiences to screaming hysteria.

Its simple emotions and mix of interweaving vocals, has made it a prototype for all boy bands, but we do not give this label to the Beatles today due to their constant artistic evolution. No sooner had it become an enormous hit than its commercial formula fell out of favour if not out of use, as none of their A-sides thereafter pandered to a teen-girl audience alone. The reasons are several. John and Paul spurred one another on to outthink the other, but they faced an external threat too. No sooner had 'I Want to Hold Your Hand' dropped out of the charts than the Rolling Stones' insolent swagger grabbed the nation's imagination by being marketed profitably as the polar opposite of clean-cut boys who sang of fidelity and how it made them all happy inside. It would become a source of discomfort at their first meeting with Bob Dylan in New York in the summer of 1964. Coasting a wave of critical approval and hip-ness, a casually-dressed Dylan visited their hotel suite and offered them marijuana for the first time. Amused at their inexperience, he asked snidely, "surely the lyrics to 'I Want to Hold Your Hand' referred to the drug, with the line 'I get high'". A star-struck John explained, as Dylan surely knew, that he was singing of a love he could not 'hide'.

Was 'I Want to Hold Your Hand' tailored to be a US No.1?

Two weeks after 'I Want to Hold Your Hand' was mixed, Brian Epstein was on a plane to Capitol Records in New York with an acetate disc in his hand luggage. Capitol was a subsidiary of EMI, the Beatles' UK label, but it only issued records it believed would sell in the US market and it had so far passed on 'Please Please Me', 'From Me To You' and 'She Loves You'. Epstein's assistant, Peter Brown, recalled the strategy was to explain how 'I Want to Hold Your Hand' had been created to suit the US market.

This was logical, as John and Paul had already successfully crafted 'From Me To You' for their UK fans. However, neither has confirmed this and George Martin has even denied it. But then it is highly probable in the three-hour session he spent producing it neither John or Paul had time to mention it. They told their biographer, Hunter Davies, that it was an attempt to write in a 'mock-American gospel' style, but the main clue is the prominent use of handclaps. In the three months leading up to the recording of 'I Want to Hold Your Hand' three out of five of the songs to hit the No.1 spot in the US had featured prominent handclaps: 'Fingertips Part 2' by Stevie Wonder, 'My Boyfriend's Back' by The Angels and 'So Much In Love' by The Tymes.

Capitol spent heavily to promote 'I Want to Hold Your Hand', though, whether this was due to Epstein's persuasion or Lennon/McCartney's tailoring is a moot point. Bruce Spizer, in his book The Beatles Are Coming – The Birth of Beatlemania in America argues that US media coverage of the group was already building momentum. In early December, a DJ in Washington played an imported copy of the single and was deluged with listeners asking to hear it again. Soon radio stations in Chicago and St Louis were getting the same response. Newspaper articles appeared and a TV broadcast of the phenomenon of Beatlemania in the UK was shown on CBS Evening News on 10th December. When Capitol eventually released 'I Want to Hold Your Hand' on 30th December there was already massive demand.

I WANT TO TELL YOU
Words: Harrison   Music: Harrison/McCartney
Originally entitled: 'I Don't Know'.
Recorded 2nd and June 3rd 1966
Found on *Revolver*

This honest admission of George's inarticulate attempts to express his thoughts was ironically one of his first powerful lyrics. It acknowledges that his previous efforts had fallen short – memorably in *Anthology* he complained of having to write his worst songs in public, while John and Paul had written theirs before they had a recording contract. Here the 'confusion' and 'hung up' feelings he sings of are expressed in the discord between Paul's piano and bass. This fits the avant-garde flavour of *Revolver*, but it lacks the appeal of 'Something' on which he reworked the same themes of inarticulate expression with a serene self-accepting melody.

I WANT YOU (SHE'S SO HEAVY)
Words: Lennon   Music: Lennon/McCartney
John lifted the main tune from the lounge music classic 'Comin'
Home Baby' by Mel Torme from 1962. Most of the lyrics come from
the chorus of Bob Dylan's 'I Want You'.
The basic track was completed on 22nd February 1969 with overdubs
on 18th and 20th April and 8th August
Found on *Abbey Road*

Much mocked for his obsessive relationship with Yoko Ono, John saw the humour in it too. His obsession, he tells us tongue-in-cheek, is driving him mad. To demonstrate, he foregoes verses and a chorus and repeats the main title phrase, 'I want you', 24 times. The joke is evoked in a spiralling guitar riff, repeatedly double-tracked.

As the most extreme of the *Abbey Road* tracks, it did not find favour with all. Chief engineer, Geoff Emerick, recalled a scene in the control room where John's instruction to overdub white noise from a Moog synthesiser, to conjure up a final descent into oblivion, left Paul burying his head in despair. He, no doubt, felt this masked the chemistry of one of their finest group performances, one of the last times they played live together. Here, they adeptly mimic the heavy blues rock that Led Zeppelin had unveiled on their debut album in January 1969. Tantalisingly, it shows them still evolving and judging by the glorious wash of colour from Billy Preston's Hammond organ, perhaps a fifth member would have been part of that journey.

I WILL

McCartney
"One of my favourite melodies," Paul '98
Recorded 16th and 17th September 1968
Found on *The Beatles* aka the White Album

A dazzling, carefree summer melody, 'I Will' owes something to the tranquillity at the meditation camp in Rishikesh, India. With hours to spend in the open air with an acoustic guitar, Paul fashioned his longest-ever chord progression – 15 chords in a row before any repetition.

The recording stayed true to its origins by being simple and acoustic, but at one minute 48 seconds it is over as soon as the listener has become acquainted with it and it has become customary for cover versions to double its length.

The lyrics which followed after returning from India undersell the melody by acting as a collection of love song clichés which suggest Paul had nothing to say on the subject at the time. The comparison with 'Julia', the following track on the album, is unflattering. Here, John sings an emotionally-charged set of words that eke every last drop out of a simpler melody. Indeed, Paul would soon return to form, inspired by his relationship with Linda

Eastman, with the affectionate 'Two Of Us' and 'Maybe I'm Amazed'. If there is any genuine love on 'I Will' it is in the devotion of John to sit on the floor playing woodblocks for 67 takes until it was perfected.

I'LL BE BACK
Lennon/McCartney
Recorded in 16 takes on 1st June 1964
Found on *A Hard Day's Night*

Playing around with the dramatic Am, G, F, E descent that opens Del Shannon's 'Runaway', John created something original. After A minor, each chord in some way previews what follows next. So, before G, there is a quick down stroke of C (the tonic note of G) and instead of an F major, John plays an F major seventh with its open high note of E, that previews the entrance of E major. This resolves to A major, teasingly introducing the returning A minor. The switch between major and minor shows two emotions: on A minor John starts with a threat to leave if his heart is broken again, but the brightness added by A major is where he sings the title phrase 'I'll Be Back'. By contrast, Shannon's verse ends on the gloom-laden and ever-resolving A minor with him still desperate to find out where his 'girl' has gone. The middle eight alludes to John's light hearted twist – even if he does leave, he says, he will be unable to stop himself returning again. In a further word-game, John even alludes to the Shannon hit (ran away).

To match the lush vocal harmonies, the Beatles took the unusual step of overdubbing an extra acoustic guitar, giving the track three in total. The words read as a message of reassurance to their UK fans before they embarked on long international tours over the summer of 1964.

I'LL BE ON MY WAY

McCartney/Lennon
Recorded live for BBC radio on 4th April 1963
First aired on radio 24th June 1963, first released on disc November 1994
Found on *Live at the BBC*

Harmonically rich and lyrically dire; John and Paul's gorgeous dual lead vocals are paired with clichéd and wooden Tin Pan Alley rhymes. Now confident hit-makers, 'I'll Be On My Way' was aired only once on radio where its lyrics would not face scrutiny, but given no release on record, showing the imperious quality control they could now exercise.

The performance shows great attention to detail for a radio recording, with a rim-shot beat and a tricky two-string solo (the laugh in Paul's voice at 1.21, as the solo finishes, hints that George has missed a note). Both these are Buddy Holly stylisations and the cheerful break-up theme is also found on 'Early in the Morning' and 'It Doesn't Matter Anymore'.

I'LL CRY INSTEAD

Lennon
Completed in eight takes on 1st June 1964
Found on *A Hard Day's Night*

John only needed the slightest encouragement to add humour to his songs. By declaring himself 'mad' and asking to be locked away, he was sending up an unintentionally hilarious line from Paul's 'A World Without Love', which was donated to the folk duo Peter and Gordon and became an international hit. He may also have been inspired by the Isley Brothers' 'I'm Laughing to Keep from Crying'. This made wicked fun of the Smokey Robinson and the Miracles' US hit 'I've Got To Dance To Keep From Crying', by creating a list of activities the singer has to perform to keep from crying, culminating in the wonderfully daft pledge that he is going to whistle to keep from crying.

For John, humour was also a guise for personal confession. Saying he has enough reasons to be crazy, tells of the tragedy he had already experienced in life. While the 'chip' on his shoulder, and how it impacted on his ability to talk to people, was a fair reflection of his belligerence when drunk, that caused many who knew him to fear his vicious tongue.

I'LL FOLLOW THE SUN

McCartney
Ringo pats his thighs instead of drums
The first version was recorded on a reel-to-reel tape recorder April-May 1960
Recorded in eight takes on 18th October 1964
Found on *Beatles For Sale*

Often criticised for its sentiments, 'I'll Follow the Sun' is more palatable when viewed as a teenager's dream of fame and travel rather than as an inability to commit when times get tough. Written when Paul was 17 it is grandly addressed to someone he expects to leave for better things. In its original form it was sweetened by the line 'Have courage, follow me, my dear' but when re-written as a 22 year-old, who had recently visited four continents, this line became a more world-weary acceptance of the loss of a friend, fitting the downbeat tone to *Beatles For Sale*.

Its simplicity and brevity at 1.44, as if the band had run out of notes, suggests the limited development of this teenage sketch. Its delicateness led to the dispensing of drums and the simple game of contrasts on vocals. Paul is at first single-tracked, then joined by John, and then double-tracked on the chorus. Originally it contained a solo played on acoustic guitar by John, however, studio engineer, Geoff Emerick, recalled a stroppy George entering the control room and pressuring George Martin to let him play the simple electric guitar line, which he improvised on the spot.

I'LL GET YOU

Lennon/McCartney
B-side to 'She Loves You'
Recorded on 1st July 1963
Found on *Past Masters*

As a boy, Andy Summers, guitarist with The Police, saw the Beatles live in 1963 and recalled Paul asking audiences to cheer for either 'She Loves You' or 'I'll Get You' to help decide which should be the next A-side single. Hearing it today, it is hard to imagine how 'I'll Get You' could ever have been in contention. Notably, vocal gaffes between 1.14 and 1.17 went uncorrected almost as if the Beatles were in a hurry to leave the studio, but the way its lyrics read as a conversation with the listener suggests a bigger plan, as does the shameless way John asks a girl to imagine he is in love with her. John would use a similar, but nobler, opening lyrical gambit on 'Imagine'.

IF I FELL

Lennon/McCartney
The recording and the creation of this arrangement was achieved from scratch in three hours.
Recorded in 15 takes on 27th February 1964
Found on *A Hard Day's Night*

A song of stark contrasts: a desire for revenge, unreasonable behaviour and deep insecurity are matched with angelic harmonies sung like choir-boys. John repeatedly asks for reassurance before entering into a relationship*, but asks the girl in question to make no such demands and simply love him 'completely'. Furthermore, he relishes the thought that if they do get together, his previous love will 'cry' on learning of this.

That John was prepared to sing it for laughs in the film *A Hard Day's Night*, where he addresses it to a grumpy Ringo, shows a measure of embarrassment at this mean-spirited utterance.

*The original notes for the lyrics reveal the unused line 'Would you know just what to do to keep me?'

IF I NEEDED SOMEONE
Harrison
George's riff was taken from the Byrds' arrangement of 'The Bells of Rhymney'.
Basic track recorded 16th October 1965 with vocals added on 18th October
Found on *Rubber Soul*

A warm melody, lush harmonies and a perfectly-executed 12-string guitar riff cannot disguise a cold emotional edge. Where on *Rubber Soul* John and Paul were taking a leap into the unknown by examining their own feelings and contrasting them with the thoughts of others, George was still trotting out the pop prince hauteur displayed six months earlier on Paul's 'Another Girl'. His only commitment to the girl in question is 'if' and 'might', which baldly contrasts the empathy and understanding of 'Nowhere Man', 'In My Life' and 'We Can Work It Out'. A somewhat mono-tonal lead vocal does not aid his case, so much so that George Martin pushes up the faders for John and Paul's vocals for equal prominence.

IN MY LIFE

Words: John   Music Lennon/McCartney
"My first real major piece of work." John '80
The basic track was recorded on 18th October 1965 with the piano
overdubbed on 22nd October.
Found on *Rubber Soul*

Stumbled upon by trial and error, while John knew he
wanted to create a message with more depth than his earlier
work, his first draft was a leaden description of Liverpool
landmarks remembered from his youth. Such panoramas
came to life for Bob Dylan because he mixed them with
fictional imagery, but John's account of trams, docks and
statues was simple and sincere. Temporarily defeated, he
lay down, where in a flash he realised that a summary of
'places' he would remember made his message universal.
It also drew on his instinct for direct and simple language.
This now made up a single verse and left room for more
memories. So a dedication to Stuart Sutcliffe, his best friend
from art school, who died aged 22, makes up the second
verse. This also references his close friend, Pete Shotton,
who witnessed the lyrics' creation and who viewed the
third verse, with its resolution as a love song, as dishonest.
Indeed, it jolts the sentiment from bittersweet to sweet, but
it serves, too, as a commitment to the present ('something
new'), a default Lennon/McCartney setting.

John appears to have drawn influence from the poem
by Charles Lamb, 'The Old Familiar Faces'. Popular in
English poetry collections, it was written in 1818 as a
remembrance of old friends and its line 'How some they
have died, and some they have left me' is starkly similar to
John's second verse. 'Bob Dylan's Dream' from the
Freewheelin' album is another pessimistic precursor. Dylan
concludes he would pay $1000 to return to the times he
spent with his old friends. 'In My Life', though, goes
further than both due to its conclusion being an affirmation
of the present, rather than a contemplation on ageing.

It was also a favourite within the group. Paul gave over a whole page of his biography to contesting John's claim to have written the melody. His recollection of writing it on a mellotron at John's house and basing it on a Smokey Robinson track is too vivid to be made up. 'Tracks of My Tears' was then in the US charts and it features a not dissimilar opening gambit of moving from G major to E minor and through to C major, a similar tempo and a spindly guitar line. Paul was not the only fan. George later played it live in his solo act, while George Martin was moved to create a little piece of wizardry by playing a piano solo at half tempo, speeding it up to the tone of a harpsichord and fitting it in the allotted two bar slot as an overdub. A great touch, too, comes from Ringo who delicately taps his way round his kit, occasionally giving way to the shake of a tambourine for the most affectionate lines.

The Creative Dead End

IT'S ONLY LOVE
Lennon/McCartney. Recorded in six takes on 15th June 1965
YOU LIKE ME TOO MUCH
Harrison. Recorded in eight takes on 17th February 1965
TELL ME WHAT YOU SEE
McCartney. Recorded in four takes on 18th February 1965
Found on tracks 8, 9 and 10 from *Help!*

The best explanation for this undistinguished run of tracks is an exhaustion of good ideas to 'pander', as Paul put it, to their girl fans. At a point of transition while exploring the uncomfortable emotions of 'You've Got to Hide Your Love Away' and 'Yesterday', they still clung to teen romance tales from the fear of moving too fast for their fans.

John despairingly recalled 'Its Only Love' as the worst thing he ever wrote. "I was so ashamed, I could hardly sing". John rhymes 'my-oh-my' with 'butterflies' in the first verse for 'It's Only Love' and its original lyric sheet reveals the depths he plummeted to complete a second and final verse. In the margin he wrote out 'mite, kite, bite, sight, invite, nite' to help him find the line where 'sight' rhymes with 'night' and 'bright'. This was carelessly close to 'Tell Me What You See' in which Paul pledges to make the day 'bright'. In front of a microphone John audibly recoils from these rhymes and at 1.06 he can be heard stifling a laugh. On any other occasion he would have gone for a second take but his instinct was to leave it, as if his lacklustre display excused him from the words.

Next up on Help! *was George's 'You Like Me Too Much' which he described as "naïve" and likewise, Paul damned 'Tell Me What You See' as "unmemorable". Both offer soporific accounts of romantic bliss backed by overly lush multi-layers of music.*

THE INNER LIGHT
Harrison
B-side to 'Lady Madonna'
The basic track was recorded by Indian musicians on 12th January 1968 at EMI studios in Bombay. Vocals were added at Abbey Road on 6th and 8th February
Found on *Past Masters*

While largely admired for its beatific harmonies, this softly spoken B-side contains a central contradiction. George quotes ancient Chinese sage, Lao-Tzu, on the wisdom of looking within oneself rather than travelling, but its recording was made on one of his quests to India, in the EMI studio in Bombay. The suggestion to put Lao-Tzu to Indian music came from Juan Mascaró, a Sanskrit scholar at Cambridge University, but the reliance on another's words highlight George's struggle to find his voice. Indeed the plaintive half-whispered vocals not only undersell the pretty tune, but make the listener feel as if they were intruding on a private recital. The contrast with Paul's universal message on the A side could not be greater.

IN SPITE OF ALL THE DANGER
McCartney
Recorded 1958
Found on *Anthology*

For a British teenager brought up in awe of all things American, aping an Elvis Presley tune was a natural first songwriting step. Written by Paul as a 16 year-old it was based on 'Trying to Get to You', its title taken from a line in one of its verses and using the same E, A, B chords. Where Elvis pledges to travel over mountains and valleys both night and day to reach his loved one, in his footsteps, Paul will do anything no matter how dangerous too.

The group, then named the Quarrymen, paid to put this on disc and John at 17, Paul 16 and George 15, (plus Colin Hanton, aged 19, on drums and Duff Lowe, aged 16, on piano), must have felt they got their money's worth. The musicianship is limited, but the bluesy authority in John's voice breathes life into the pallid lyrics, as does Paul's, by joining John on key words such as 'heartbreak' and 'danger' – an early sign of the harmonies that would make them famous.

IT'S ALL TOO MUCH

Harrison
Written from "realisations made from LSD" George '80.
A backing track was recorded on 25th May 1967 with overdubs added
on 26th May and 2nd June
Found on *Yellow Submarine*

Sweetly-sung lines about a universal love help make the coda to the *Yellow Submarine* film one of its most powerful scenes. Its message fits the cartoon's child-like world view in a way that George had probably not intended. As he recalled the lyrics were inspired by the 'liberating' effects of LSD and like 'Tomorrow Never Knows' and 'Fixing A Hole' it compares this to floating on a stream.

The recording, without George Martin, who was on holiday, was chaotic. Trumpet player, David Mason, recalled: "George was in charge of that session, I don't think he really knew what he wanted". The mix of Jimi Hendrix-style feedback with brass (this was recorded in the same studio Hendrix frequented) suggests George wanted to emulate the same mix found on 'Sgt.Pepper's Lonely Hearts Club Band'.

IT WON'T BE LONG

Lennon/McCartney
The word 'yeah' is sung 55 times here. 'She Loves You' by
comparison has 'yeah' sung only 29 times.
Recorded in 23 takes on 30th July 1963
Found on *With The Beatles*

Welding together the best bits of their most popular songs must have seemed an interesting idea when looking for a new hit. So here, the same promise of everlasting fidelity of 'From Me To You' is matched with the noise and fever of 'Twist And Shout'. Ultimately, when it was recorded, 'She Loves You' was already in the frame, and by comparison 'It Won't Be Long''s word-game of 'be long' and 'belong' is a weak artifice. One idea both had in common was their ending. Here the hysteria elegantly collapses with 7th chords (concluding on a mellow Emaj7) which not only suggests sleep after a busy day, but also segues nicely into the mellow, jazzy opening of the next track 'All I've Got To Do'.

JULIA

Lennon
John's first love song since 1965.
Recorded 13th October 1968
Found on *The Beatles* aka The White Album

John's instinct was to communicate with his audience by making his words universal, but occasionally he wrote for himself alone. This conversation with his mother, Julia, who died in a car accident 10 years earlier, makes the listener feel as if they are intruding on his grief. He measures the pain of his loss by estimating that half of what he says was driven by a need to reach out to her. Using voice and guitar alone with the minimum of production effects, it does not seek a wider audience by being sweetened or made easy listening with orchestration. Other than a little double-tracking, it is a rare hearing of John's voice with an absence of echo or reverberation.

Started during spells of meditation in India, the first draft contained the line 'her hair like saffron shimmering, glimmering', a reference to his mother's auburn hair. Once back home the line was changed to a reference to 'floating sky', words from one of Yoko Ono's letters which read that she was a cloud and if John looked into the sky he would be able to see her. So his mother became intertwined with Yoko Ono, who, seven years his senior, was quickly becoming an alternative mother-figure. The imagery from her letters, the sand, sea, moon and sky, was used to conjure up both her and his mother's presence. While this twist might seem to lessen the tribute, it is entirely in keeping with his instincts. The remembrance of Stuart Sutcliffe in 'In My Life' similarly evolved into a dedication to current friends and lovers – John's loyalty was always to the present and the future.

KANSAS CITY

Little Richard's version of Leiber and Stoller's 'Kansas City' was merged with his 'Hey-Hey-Hey' composition.
Recorded in one take on 18th October 1964
Found on *Beatles For Sale*

Keen to save time in a busy schedule, John goaded Paul into giving a storming performance on the very first take. Its normal purpose was a rousing shout-along that went down well in packed nightclubs and the 'Hey-Hey-Hey' section shows the interaction the group must have enjoyed with their fans.

LADY MADONNA

McCartney
Derived from 'Bad Penny Blues' a trad jazz tune and a hit for Humphrey Lyttleton in 1956.
First released as a single on 15th March 1968
A backing track of Paul on piano and Ringo on drums was recorded on 3rd February 1968 with John and George's guitars overdubbed next. The brass was added on 6th February.
Found on *Past Masters*

Championing women would have been an odd departure from the chauvinistic values of the Sixties' rock world, and as if conscious of this, Paul's tribute to the all-hours work his mother put in as a midwife is not entirely convincing. The imagery is ambivalent and sugar-coated with an old fashioned boogie-woogie, an approach soon repeated to soften the politics of 'Revolution 1'. Rather than any social message the lasting impression is of the fun had in the comical scat vocals and a frantic piano finger exercise. The leaping bass lines and deep-toned vocal were styled on Fats Domino, as were the lyrics which borrow from 'Blue Monday'. Where Domino charts a man's hard work throughout the week with his day of rest on Saturday, Paul uses the days of the week to chart the tribulations of his heroine, though for her, pointedly, Saturday never comes. It is believed 'Across the Universe' was originally intended as the A-side from these sessions, so whilst strong, 'Lady Madonna' lacks the usual X factor of the typical Beatles' single and only managed No. 4 in the US charts.

LEAVE MY KITTEN ALONE
Written by Little Willie John/James McDougal and Titus Turner
Recorded in five takes on 14th August 1964
Found on *Anthology I*

Was embarrassment at forgetting lyrics the reason this was held back from release for 30 years? John's searing vocal gives it more life than many of the tracks chosen for *Beatles For Sale*, but the Johnny Preston original contains an extra line in the chorus and an extra verse. Having not performed it on stage for well over a year it is very possible John forgot them. Otherwise Preston's arrangement has more of a novelty feel with female vocals singing 'miaow' throughout, as does the original by Little Willie John. Here there is menace rather than humour – a version which must have gone down well live.

LET IT BE
McCartney
"One night during this tense time I had a dream, I saw my mum who had been dead ten years or so. In the dream she said: 'It'll be alright'.

I'm not sure she used the words 'Let It Be', but that was the gist of her advice." Paul '98

Main recording completed 31st January 1969, guitar solo overdubbed 4th January1970.

Found on *Let It Be*

The misery of group in-fighting led Paul to seek solace in the memory of his dead mother. Bickering and mistrust had made friends into enemies and here his world-weariness is played out in flat, major chords. The first introduction of a minor chord comes on the mention of his mother Mary, where his voice wavers on a high note. His recollection of his mother telling him not to worry, recalls 'Julia', which tells of John's mother talking to him whilst he was in a dream-like state.

Never one to dwell on personal unhappiness, Paul pushed himself to find uplift for the second verse, where he imagines how his mother's advice could be of use to the world's broken-hearted, which speaks volumes for the song's enduring popularity. Uplift is also found in George's free-ranging guitar solo which hints at a salvation the lyrics do not state.

Paul placed the tune in a black gospel setting with piano and vocals to the fore. That Mary shared her name with the mother of Jesus makes this all the more fitting. Indeed, Paul gave it to the soul and gospel singer, Aretha Franklin, whose version appeared before the Beatles'.

LET IT BE (Album)

Album released 8th May 1970

Rehearsed 2nd-23rd January, recorded 24th-31st January 1969

Let It Be was designed to be a dazzling coup and a benchmark for others. A live album of new songs filmed at the point of recording that would showcase their musical chemistry and wit. In practice, the goodwill needed to achieve this had evaporated and bad planning worsened everyone's mood. The project kicked off on 2nd January, the most unpopular and least productive day in the working year. The early morning starts, the cold and the cavernous setting of a TV studio, with rivers of cable and cameramen surrounding them created what John later described as a "dreadful feeling".

John himself was little help. A heroin-induced lethargy left him openly bored with contributing to anything that was not his or at least co-written. To fill this vacuum, Paul increasingly organised and chivvied the group. For George, this was the final straw. After seven days of aimless jams, half-hearted cover versions and unpromising stabs at rehearsing new songs, he snapped and walked. This split forced everyone to come to their senses and move to the cosy basement of their central London office. Here, George wisely introduced Hammond organ virtuoso, Billy Preston, to the rehearsals. He brought a fuller sound and forced John to put on a better show of himself. Relief at escaping the TV studio and at George's return led to fun, breezy tracks, ('I've Got A Feeling', 'For You Blue' and 'I Dig a Pygmy') being favoured, whilst the solemnity of 'All Things Must Pass' and a remake of 'Across The Universe' were side-stepped, only Paul tempting fate by forcing a visibly miserable group through 'Let It Be' and 'The Long and Winding Road'. Over a ten-day period 10 songs were brought to life – just enough to fill an album.

A tug of war – the story of the *Let It Be* releases

The first official mix of Let It Be owes itself to the impatient pragmatism of John, the second to the attention to detail of Paul. In February 1970, after a year of disagreement over what to do with the tapes, which all knew to be unsatisfactory, John, in a fait accompli, instructed them to be handed over to Phil Spector, the legendary producer of the Ronettes and the Righteous Brothers. As well as impatience, John had the motive of wanting to see some magic worked on his flawed but beautiful 'Across the Universe', which had lacked an official Beatles' release for two years.

Spector was best known for his 'wall of sound' achieved through duplication of instruments and string sections and he duly added violins and choirs to 'Let It Be', 'The Long and Winding Road' and 'Across the Universe'. Paul was horrified, but as Spector said in his defence, the Beatles were already ashamed of the tapes and he was making the best of a bad job. In this form Let It Be was released in May 1970, but such was Paul's disgust he cited his unhappiness with these overdubs in the High Court as one of the reasons the Beatles' business partnership should end. A full thirty years later, he was the driving force in taking advantage of new technology to have the tapes remixed as Let It Be Naked. Here the overdubs were removed and some instruments previously buried in the mix can now be heard clearly. The cleaned-up versions of 'The Long and Winding Road' and 'Across the Universe' are its biggest triumphs.

LIKE DREAMERS DO
McCartney/ Lennon
HELLO LITTLE GIRL
Lennon/McCartney
Both recorded in single takes on 1st January 1962
First official release 1995
Found on *Anthology 1*

Before they became adept writers, John and Paul honed songs over months and years, rather than discard them. So, four years after they had been created, at the ages of 17 and

16, final touches were still being applied to 'Love of the Loved' and 'Hello Little Girl'. It was hoped the changes would impress the record companies they were now courting, but their effort comes across as desperation and their passion is fake – particularly in the way each song repeats a word three times ('love, love, love', 'you, you, you') for emphasis. In the same spirit, Paul sang 'Love of The Loved' at the Decca sessions in a tone deeper than normal, as if unconfident the record label would be impressed with his natural voice. His strident performance is matched by Pete Best's pneumatic drum fills which give a zip that the corny drama did not deserve. On 'Hello Little Girl' John, as a 21 year-old, is similarly all at sea with a set of words written by a teenager. They learnt quickly from this disaster and started new material in earnest. Only eight months later they had written what would become their first number one hit, 'Please Please Me'.

LITTLE CHILD
Lennon/McCartney
Paul lifted the melancholic chord change on the word 'lonely' from a score to an old Robin Hood film.
Recorded in 18 takes between 11th-12th September 1963
Found on *With the Beatles*

If there is any doubt as to who was the true leader of the Beatles, John here stepped into the breach after Ringo refused to sing this. Dismissed by its writers as made without love in order to fill up the album, John gives a super-human performance to bring emotion to a set of inconsequential lyrics and a repetitive melody. His scream mid-song and his harmonica playing are produced as if this was the finest tune performed at the Cavern on a Friday night.

A LITTLE HELP FROM MY FRIENDS

Music: McCartney   Lyrics: McCartney/Lennon
After Ringo achieved the final high note John, Paul and George all broke out into cheers.
Basic track recorded 29th March 1967 with overdubs on 30th March
Found on *Sgt. Pepper's Lonely Hearts Club Band*

Rare is the lyric that eulogises the happiness shared by members of a pop group. Rarer still is one written out of affection for a drummer. Sweetly, Paul's lyrics, with help from John, state the group's friendship is as durable and as important as any wife or girlfriend. Written in the warm glow of satisfaction as *Sgt. Pepper's* approached completion, it is a rare break from the album's fantastical themes. It is also a thank-you to Ringo who spent so many hours patiently waiting while overdubs were recorded and sound balances tinkered with and gave him his moment to shine, with the task of hitting his highest-ever vocal note at the close.

The first verse tells of his self-consciousness at singing lead and John joins in the gentle mocking by writing the third verse which required him to make a veiled allusion to masturbation. John, though, was sincere about the chorus and later defended it from the popular belief it was about drugs – as he later emphasised, the main message was truly about friendship. Great encouragement was given to Ringo to get his vocal right, although he is not required to carry the tune alone as the backing vocals take most of the high notes. It seems probable that the Motown stylisation – the rhythm guitar plays across the beat, rather than on it – was done to find a style Ringo was comfortable with.

LIVE AT THE BBC
Recorded for BBC radio between January 1963 and May 1965.
Album first released 30th November 1994

Fresh from their time as a seven day a week club band, these tapes reveal glimpses of the early Beatles as an attraction that sold out venues with the captivating draw of improving on American pop songs.

'Sweet Little Sixteen' is one of its gems. Here the stop-start riff is transformed by the twin attack of John and George's guitars, while a judicious edit of the verses leaves it half a minute leaner than the original, whilst its improvised guitar solo is a revelation. The original has a piano solo, so free of any expectations George lets loose with a string of Chuck Berry-like licks all crammed into one 22 second fire burst.

Another triumph is 'Don't Ever Change', which is made faster and warmer than the Crickets' hit by George's vocals being supported by Paul for greater persuasion. Elsewhere, Chan Romero's weird shamanistic rocker 'Hippy Hippy Shake' is extended from 1.39 to 1.50, to make it more mainstream, its inexplicable line 'it's in the bag' becoming 'Oh my babe'.

Yet more invention is found on Little Richard's 'Lucille' – an improvised guitar solo is joined by a line dreamt up by Paul: 'Lucille, baby, satisfy my soul, well you know I love you baby and I'll never let you go'. No doubt on marathon club nights, embellishments were made and from numerous try outs of 'Lonesome Tears in My Eyes', John learnt to bring a power and clarity missing from the hillbilly mumble of Johnny Burnette.

There are curios too. John's edgy reading of 'Honey Don't' is a revelation compared to Ringo's sorry take on *Beatles for Sale*, while there is a bunch of spirited, if misguided, Elvis covers, where John, Paul and George queue up to emulate their hero, but never match his regal baritone.

On 3rd August 1963 the Beatles played the Cavern for the last time and thereafter a familiarity with their live repertoire faded. The nadir was reached on the May 1965 radio session at which a forced and inauthentic 'Dizzy Miss Lizzie' was made. Turning out inferior imitations of songs they had once owned must have been dispiriting and they subsequently rejected all requests to appear live on radio.

THE LONG AND WINDING ROAD

McCartney
"I like writing sad songs…because you can acknowledge some deeper feelings of your own…it saves have to go to a psychiatrist." Paul '98
Recorded in seven takes on 31st January 1969, with Phil Spector's overdubs added on 1st April 1970
Found on *Let It Be*

This is surely the bleakest Beatles' song. Unlike the detached, distant pain of 'For No One' or 'Yesterday', the moment Paul placed his fingers on the piano keys to sketch out its first lines he was in a squall of depression. Whilst he had the instinct for a pretty melody, his words contain no joy at this creation. Wearily they trudge out, as though worn down by the bickering with his sharp-tongued band mate, John. Paul described it as an act of psychoanalysis and for some its soul-searching reads as a call to religion, with its request to be shown the 'way'*, but it makes more sense if seen as a plea for an escape from his predicament, one he would find when writing 'Let It Be' days later. Both contain the request not to be left alone. The first seeks the way from a parent-figure, or a god, and the second receives an answer from the spirit of his dead mother. Notably where 'The Long and Winding Road' tells of night, wind, rain and tears, on 'Let It Be', there is a light shining out of this darkness. Both were written in the autumn of 1968 in Paul's hideaway in the Kintyre peninsula in Scotland, which is reached on a long, winding sea road.

Paul cited Ray Charles as an influence and his mournful 'Don't Let the Sun Catch You Crying' also has 'door' as a metaphor for openness. Both refer to weather and where Ray Charles urges the listener not to cry during the daytime, Paul refers to crying at night. Tellingly, he was captured playing Ray Charles's tune during the *Let It Be* sessions.

A deeply personal song, Paul was appalled at the lush overdubs given to it by Phil Spector; the addition of strings and a choir is a softening touch which sweetens his personal crisis. Such was his anger he cited this interference to the High Court, in London in 1970, as cause for the Beatles' business partnership to end. Thirty three years later Paul got his way and a stripped-down version was released on *Let It Be...Naked*.

*In the film *It's a Wonderful Life* the main character, George Bailey, as played by James Stewart utters 'show me the way' three times while sitting in Martini's wine bar praying silently and contemplating taking his own life.

LONG LONG LONG

Harrison
A basic track of drums – Ringo, acoustic guitar – George and organ – Paul recorded 7th October 1968 with overdubs on 8th and 9th October
Found on *The Beatles* aka The White Album

The search for a god or a universal love proved a rich seam of inspiration for George. 'Within You Without You', 'The Inner Light', 'While My Guitar Gently Weeps' and 'My Sweet Lord' and 'Long, Long, Long' are some of his most soulful tunes and here he creates a luscious melancholy that at times says more in mood than word. The way each word of the chorus is given a different emphasis is not far off Bob Dylan's impenetrable mood-piece, 'Sad-Eyed Lady of The Lowlands', from which George borrowed the same D, Em, A chord pattern. This dedication to mood led to the eccentric ending where a rattle competes with a ghostly wail. The noise was caused by a bottle resting on a Hammond organ that vibrated each time a note of high resonance was played.

LONG TALL SALLY

Written by Richard Penniman (Little Richard), Robert 'Bumps' Blackwell and Enotris Johnson
Recorded in one take on 1st March 1964
Found on *Past Masters*

From playing church halls in Liverpool as the Quarrymen, right up until the final world tour of 1966, the Beatles would favour ending the evening with their fastest number. This was not only a piece of showmanship but a sales pitch. The pace of 'Long Tall Sally' not only left the audience high, but told them of the 'fun' they were having 'tonight'. Its ferocious speed, so legend has it, came from Little Richard's desire to put off white crooner, Pat Boone, from covering it – Boone had riled him by finding greater commercial success with 'Tutti Frutti' than he had.

The Beatles probably performed it 1000 times live, so one studio take was all it needed. Indeed, such was their familiarity with it, they delivered a performance many prefer to the original, not least for George's solo, which honed over years, is masterful in ratcheting up the speed and tension. Richard's version from 1956 relies more on salacious insinuation than power. Notably, Paul drops the homosexual innuendo of 'bald-headed Sally', simply singing this as 'long tall sally'. Another tidied-up line was 'built for speed', which becomes 'built pretty sweet'.

LOVE
Album first released 20th November 2006

Does this count as a genuine Beatles product? Is it any good? 'Love' should perhaps be renamed 'love it or hate it' for the way it has divided fans who either enjoy the surprise of its mash-ups or deplore it as an artificial enterprise without the sanction of each Beatle. Whilst its experimentation is in keeping with the group's ethos, it is in fact a remix album done with great input from an outside producer – Giles Martin, the son of George Martin.

LOVE ME DO
McCartney/Lennon
John plays a harmonica stolen from a music shop in Arnhem, Holland.
"I can still hear the shake in my voice when I listen to that record – I was terrified. John did sing it better than me, he had a lower voice and was much more bluesy at singing that line." Paul '88
Two versions recorded on 4th September and 11th September 1962
Found on *Past Masters* and *Please Please Me*

Nervous of the recording studio, 'Love Me Do' plods out with little of the exuberance of their next few singles. There are flashes of brilliance: the uncanny way John and Paul's voices merge on the word 'please', the syncopation of the harmonica and Paul's bluesy wail on the fade out, but it should have been better. John normally led the chorus and his voice would have been capable of delivering the words 'love me do' with menace, sexual insinuation or vulnerability. However, George Martin's first thoughts were to mould the group with a front man and he identified Paul for this role and so asked him to sing. He broke this to the group by reasoning John could not play harmonica and sing the chorus, but this was not strictly true, as the harmonica could have been overdubbed. The interference also stemmed from Martin's initial coolness for the song, a reaction shared by the London media who gave it a muted reception. Yet both were out of touch, as in a prim world of state-run radio stations with conservative play lists it stood out for its looseness, which said more in feeling than words. It was all the more original for being a blues song sung in an English accent; both Mick Jagger and Keith Richards recalled feeling "sick" at being beaten to this breakthrough, as while a live sensation then, the Rolling Stones did not have a recording contract. Similarly, the media were caught by surprise at its chart placing at No.17, which led to a popular rumour that Brian Epstein had 'bought' it into charts, by forging return slips at his record shop in Liverpool. As intriguing as this is, it has been denied so adamantly by former assistants of Epstein, who now have nothing to lose from telling it, that it must be untrue.

'Love Me Do' was a work in progress for years. Written by Paul around 1958 with added help from John, it was given a make-over to prepare it for recording, principally with the addition of John's harmonica riff which he based on Bruce Chanel's hit 'Hey Baby'.

LOVE YOU TOO

Harrison
"I'm not a Beatle anymore", reported words from George Harrison after the last formal live performance by the Beatles in Candlestick Park, San Francisco, August 1966.
The basic track was recorded on 11th April 1966 with overdubs added on 13th April
Found on *Revolver*

Often described as gods, this was one of the first times the Beatles sought to sound as such. John had requested a vocal like the Dalai Lama's chanting on a mountain on 'Tomorrow Never Knows', so a week later George took advantage of newly-available automatic double-tracking and heavy echo to make his voice appear all knowing and powerful too. Microphones placed unusually close to the

A murky set of events

At the Beatles' recording test in June 1962, George Martin felt Pete Best was not up to scratch and, as the story goes, he told Brian Epstein a session drummer would be used on their first proper recording session. In what is generally believed to be a reaction to this, Pete Best was sacked from the group in August and replaced by Ringo Starr. George Martin was not told of this change, but inexplicably, no session drummer was booked for the 4th September session at which a version of 'Love Me Do' was recorded with Ringo. A week later, the group returned to Abbey Road to record with a session drummer, Andy White, who played on another version of 'Love Me Do' while Ringo played maracas. More used to playing with dance orchestras, White gave a rigid beat, at odds with the blues feel. In its favour, though, this version features a more confident vocal from Paul and was the one Martin preferred. In some kind of mix-up, early pressings of the single featured the version with Ringo from 4th September, while later pressings and the debut album used the Andy White version. Another mystery is the role of Ron Richards for the 11th September session – George Martin is popularly associated with this stage of the Beatles' story, but for some reason, Richards acted as producer. He remained largely silent on this role until his death.

tabla drums added a general heaviness of tone, which matches the solemn references to death and sin, but much of the lyrics are lighter than this. On paper they state a happy, hippy manifesto of making love and singing all day, with the moral that one should enjoy life in the present. The sour, uncommercial way George expressed himself reflected the growingly dysfunctional nature of his role in the group. Increasingly subordinate to its two main songwriters' ambitions, he found it harder to be as enthusiastic about the group as they were.

LOVELY RITA

McCartney

The first parking meters in London were placed in Manchester Square in 1958. This was the site of the Beatles' recording company headquarters, EMI.

"I had been nicked quite a lot for parking, so the fun was to imagine one of them (parking wardens) was an easy lay," Paul '98.

Parking warden, Meta Davies, claimed she was Paul's inspiration after she gave his car a ticket and he noticed how her name sounded like parking meter. 'Meter-maid', however, is North American slang.

The backing was recorded on 23rd February 1967, with overdubs on 24th February, 7th March and 21st March

Found on *Sgt. Pepper's Lonely Hearts Club Band*

Paul's first intentions were a smutty revenge satire on the growth of parking wardens in London, but at some point he found it more fun to serenade them. Rita is mocked for wearing a masculine uniform and is urged to lighten her military image by giving a wink. She even makes up for fining Paul by paying for dinner. To add further indignity, the trumpet noises that herald her were made by blowing through combs wrapped in shiny old-fashioned toilet paper. Yet the blissful vocals on the intro and the dreamily-textured chorus seem to suggest Rita should be worshipped instead. John added to the silliness with his scat singing, tripping out on the percussive lyrics, which are filled full of hard 'ter' and 'ker' sounds, at the close. However, he was left exasperated by Paul's tale, later citing it as the key difference between him and his partner: where he preferred to write about real experience Paul was happy to create fictional characters.

LUCY IN THE SKY WITH DIAMONDS

Lennon/McCartney

"[Lucy was] the image of this female who would someday come save me." John '80

'And what enormous flowers they must be!' words uttered by Alice in *Through the Looking Glass*.

This was rehearsed at Abbey Road on 28th February 1967, a backing track was recorded on 1st March, with overdubs added on 2nd March Found on *Sgt. Pepper's Lonely Hearts Club Band*

A song for his son? A code for LSD? A nursery rhyme? These are all popular interpretations of John's lyrics, but the plaintive yearning of the opening arpeggio makes a paean to the woman he wanted to meet the most convincing explanation. Lucy is the sort of figure that might have occurred in a dream. She is there at the end of a train journey waiting at a turnstile. And with sun coming from her eyes she calls to him from the banks of a river while he is on a magical boat ride past towering tangerine-coloured flowers.

John's starting point was his three year-old son's picture of a class-mate named Lucy, who is depicted flying through the sky against a background of diamond-shaped stars. The idea of a woman with special powers evoked the idealised person he wanted to meet. The setting is partly *Alice in Wonderland/ Through the Looking Glass* and partly hallucinogenic visions of landscapes and colours. The references to 'high' and having one's head in the clouds are text-book code for the psychedelic experience, as are the mentions of travel – boat, taxi, train – which state Lucy/ John/ the listener is taking a trip. Emphasising this detachment from reality, his voice has been speeded up, phased and echoed to make it like one from a dream. Only months previously, US hippie band, Jefferson Airplane, released 'White Rabbit' which also made an unashamed link between the imagery of *Alice In Wonderland* and the effects of LSD.

Many have come to see John's title as a coded reference to the drug too, a claim he strenuously denied. Indeed, the words do not spell out LSD, but LITSWD.

Paul rose to the occasion by playing the main arpeggio on organ, using a celeste key, so acutely enhanced it is always a surprise to hear. His bass, too, adds to the mood, sleep-walking around the arrangement, in the style of music found in Hollywood suspense films, while George's sitar adds a layer of exoticism by following John's vocal line, a trick he learnt from Hindustani music. This rich tapestry was achieved despite the limitations of four-track recording, by queuing up each instrument for a turn. So, where the organ plays the first half of each verse, the guitar plays for the second half, as both were sharing one of the four precious recording channels. The chorus created by Paul rudely breaks this spell. Its Salvation Army bass drum wakes the listener from sleep and it is this which probably led to John to describe the track in hindsight as 'abysmal'. Whilst a treat for the listener only he was aware of how he wanted it to sound.

MAGGIE MAE

Writer unknown
Recorded live 24th January 1969
Found on *Let It Be*

John often amused himself by singing the Beatles' old stage favourites whenever rehearsals for the *Let It Be* sessions stagnated. These were rarely complete as he could not remember all the chords or lyrics. The lines for this old sea-shanty, which he had sung as early as 1957, should read: 'I was paid off at the pool in the port of Liverpool, three pounds ten a week that was my pay, with a bucket full of tin, I was very soon taken in, by a gal with the name of Maggie May'.

Originally a nineteenth-century tale of a prostitute who robbed sailors of their pay and clothes, many versions evolved to place its setting in Bristol, Glasgow, Liverpool, London and Swansea. John is believed to have based his version on that released by the Viper Skiffle Group, yet where John sings 'dirty Maggie May', the London-based group sang 'Maggie, Maggie May'. His exaggerated Liverpool accent brought an earthiness not hinted at by the Vipers.

MAGICAL MYSTERY TOUR EP
Released 8th December 1967
Recorded in 142 hours mixed in 47 hours

Making a film and recording the soundtrack at the same time is one Beatles' precedent that has been ignored. Acting, directing, producing and editing a TV special, whilst writing and recording music, spread their talents too thinly and gave an unsatisfactory result all round. However, naive optimism was in the air in the 'summer of love' in 1967 and for some young people a new era had dawned in which Western societies' norms would change rapidly. So here too traditional instruments were put aside, distorted and synthetic sounds favoured and accepted song-writing practice dispensed with. The pragmatic advice of George Martin had little place among such light-headedness, so much so that he described a schism between the group and himself on these sessions. This attitude provides a theme of sorts, with an importance placed on questioning conformity and connecting with our dreams. Its key-note 'Fool on the Hill' was a defence of those whose imaginations are beyond the everyday. Being the Beatles, while the end result is sub-par by their own standards it is still a great work.

MAGICAL MYSTERY TOUR
Music: McCartney   Words: McCartney/ Lennon
"[Paul] gestured a lot with his hands and shouted 'Flash, Flash,' saying it would be like a commercial." Hunter Davies, '68.
Basic track recorded 25th April 1967, overdubs added 26th, 27th April and 3rd May
Found on *Magical Mystery Tour*

An advertising jingle for the alternative lifestyles being pioneered in San Francisco, Paul wrote this after a revelatory holiday in California in April 1967. There he heard of the legendary journey taken by the author, Ken Kesey, across America whilst taking and sharing LSD with all whom he met – a journey later immortalised in Tom Wolfe's book *The Electric Kool-Aid Acid Test*. Paul gave the journey a British context by framing memories of 'mystery tour' coaches that would take pensioners from Liverpool on surprise trips, usually to the seaside. This mix of old-fashioned and modern is matched by trumpets which herald the call to board the coach, but the jazzy dissonant piano hints at the altered state of drugs, a motif also used on 'Tomorrow Never Knows'. Whilst bold, it has not aged well. Arguably, the group had enough magic without labelling their work as such. Embarrassed, John blamed Paul for the idea. Not wishing to take all the blame Paul was insistent it was written on a 50/50 basis.

MARTHA MY DEAR

McCartney
Recorded 4th and 5th October 1968
Found on *The Beatles* aka The White Album

The words here were secondary to a challenging piano exercise, but ended up giving away more than intended. To keep his spirits up whilst perfecting a difficult set of tempo and key changes at home, Paul sang in a comical fashion to his sheepdog, Martha. The words he formed mourned a failed relationship. It has become a popular theory that Paul's repeated plea (in the song's last words) that he does not want to be forgotten, were unwittingly aimed at Jane Asher who had left him four months before. Paul has done nothing to deny this, going so far in his official biography to say the words probably had a deeper meaning.

The 'silly girl' section was written earlier in India,

which explains the contrasting moods in the music, which, on each change of tempo, go from sad to frivolous and back again, which is where it ends, the last notes plodding out like a slowing heartbeat.

The recording came at a time of tension and Paul appears to have thought better of forcing a fractious group through a difficult set of time-signatures for what was ostensibly an ode to his dog. So he played drums, bass, piano and guitar, only calling on George Martin to orchestrate the strings.

MATCHBOX

Unknown original writer, with changes made by Carl Perkins
"I'm ugly but nice, but they (John, Paul and George) are beautiful but terrible." Ringo, talking to a French journalist in June 1965.
Recorded in five takes on 1st June 1964
Found on *Past Masters*

A dirt-poor upbringing in Tennessee helped Carl Perkins give this tale of a down-on-his-luck traveller real bite. Ringo, in his doleful manner, sucks all the menace from it, unwittingly doing the Perkins' brand an injustice from which it still suffers. This is unfortunate for listeners and for Perkins alike as John originally sang this and his natural belligerence would have made it credible.

The origins of 'Matchbox' are obscure. Blind Lemon Jefferson's 'Matchbox Blues' from 1927 was the first famous version, after which it became both a blues and Country and Western standard, constantly rewritten with coded phrases alluding to sex and being down on one's luck. The only line from Perkins' version consistent with 'Matchbox Blues' is: 'I'm sitting here wonderin', will a matchbox hold my clothes, I ain't got no matches but I still got a long way to go'. The Beatles, in turn, changed these lines to the nonsensical 'watching a matchbox hold my clothes'. Perkins, who was in London on tour, was invited to Abbey Road studios to witness the recording. Nervous of his hero's presence George's solo is ham-fisted and jolly compared with Perkins' spidery original and George Martin judiciously buried it in the mix.

MAXWELL'S SILVER HAMMER
McCartney
Yoko Ono was lying on a double bed in the studio when this was recorded after she had injured her back in a car crash.
"Music for grannies to dig", John '80.
Basic track recorded 9th July 1969, overdubs on 10th, 11th July and 6th August
Found on *Abbey Road*

While the painstaking recording of Paul's account of a psychopath who bashes in the skulls of those who annoy him was being made, John's anti-war anthem 'Give Peace a Chance' was high in the charts. The gulf could not be greater. One was a dark nursery rhyme made with precision, the other a speedily-created message of hope. Like members of a dysfunctional family, neither John nor Paul was collaborating much anymore before they brought new songs into the studio. This forced them to endure hours perfecting compositions for which they had no ownership and which at times they came to hate. John tetchily recalled Paul making the group record 'Maxwell's Silver Hammer' a "hundred million times" in an effort to make it good enough to be a single. There is some substance to this, as it was played at the end of *The Beatles'* sessions in October 1968, rehearsed on four days of the *Let It Be* project, and another four days during the recording of *Abbey Road*.

The 1920s' styling owes much to the vaudeville pastiche of the Bonzo Dog Doo-Dah Band's 'I Am the Urban Spaceman'. Paul had produced the Bonzo's only hit just weeks before he first demo-ed 'Maxwell' and both share a surprise ending in their tale. Finished just weeks before John informed Paul of his decision to leave the group, it is popularly assumed that the conflict caused by 'Maxwell' was pivotal in the split and John's desire to put an end to the Lennon/McCartney songwriting credit.

MEAN MR MUSTARD (See page 177)

MICHELLE
Music: McCartney   Words: McCartney/ Lennon
"Notre prochaine chanson, qui s'appele 'I'm A Loser'." Months before recording 'Michelle', Paul learnt some French phrases for use at the Beatles' concerts in Paris, June 1965.
Recorded on 3rd November 1965
Found on *Rubber Soul*

Taking a day off from being themselves, the Beatles took on the guise of a French band playing in a smoky Paris night club. Under Paul's direction, they spent nine hours at Abbey Road perfecting this. In the manner of singers such as Edith Piaf, the vocals were pushed high against a muted jazz backing while the tone on the guitar solo was switched so high to reverb and bass it sounds not dissimilar to an accordion. The desire for authenticity went as far as getting a French teacher to help with the lyrics and for Paul's diction. Jan Vaughan, the wife of Paul's childhood friend, Ivan, was asked to think of a girl's name and two words that rhymed with it. This formed the first line, while Paul's request for words that went together well provided the basis for the second line. Acknowledging this input, Jan Vaughan later received a cheque from the group.

John suggested the repeated 'I love you' section which he had heard Nina Simone improvise on her version of 'I Put a Spell on You'. Curiously, the B-side for this was a French language song, a version of Jacques Brel's 'Ne Me Quitte Pas'.

Paul had the basis for the tune for around six or seven years. It started as an imitation of the guitar instrumental 'Trambone' by Chet Atkins, with a French lilt added to it and had been used as a musical joke to impress girls at the art school parties he was invited to by John as a teenager. Tapes of this instrumental show how slick he must have appeared, though Paul would mouth nonsense French over the top for laughs and it must have impressed John, as it was he who jogged Paul's memory when searching for new ideas for *Rubber Soul*.

MISERY
Lennon/McCartney
Recorded in 11 takes on 11th February 1963
Found on *Please Please Me*

There are few Lennon/McCartney artefacts lost to posterity, but the version of 'Misery' presented to Helen Shapiro in January 1963 would have had a different opening couplet to the one here where 'guy' rhymes with 'cry'. John and Paul hoped it would build their reputation if Shapiro recorded it, even as a B-side, but her management turned it down and did not hold onto the tape. Put together in the week before a national tour on which Shapiro was headlining and the Beatles supporting, its simple but swooping melody was tailored for her big, expressive voice, and its maudlin, put-upon theme is the same as those of two of her biggest hits, 'Don't Treat Me Like A Child' and 'You Don't Know'. Possibly if Shapiro's producer and Svengali, Norrie Paramour, had accepted it the Beatles might never have recorded it.

Their performance here suggests not. In the studio they were boyishly unable to treat lyrics written for a woman with any level of seriousness. The glee in John's voice mocks his sad fictional tale and after a vocal gaffe from Paul at 1.22, he can be heard stifling a laugh. Such carelessness extends to the music where the opening guitar chord is out of tune. This inability to take disappointment seriously was at the heart of the band's early appeal; for them dwelling in unhappiness was a source of hilarity.

MONEY

Written by Janie Bradford and Berry Gordy
Recorded by both the Rolling Stones and the Beatles
Recorded in seven takes on 18th July 1963, piano overdub 30th July
Found on *With the Beatles*

'Now give me money!' is not a lyric normally associated with Lennon/McCartney, but it is different from the words 'I need money' used on the original by Barrett Strong from 1959. The song was a drily amusing account of the financial dire straits Berry Gordy faced after he had quit his job at a car plant in order to set up the Motown label with an $800 loan. Transferred to a stage in Liverpool and played at high volume to teenagers in sweaty rooms it became an effective ploy for John to change the words to a demand for money rather than a request. Indeed, so hysterical is his tone, it tells of the escape the audience could have if only they had excess money too. For John, who had never held down a conventional 9-5 job, the plea was personal. His maniacal tone is matched with a grand production. Where the original's muted piano and guitar riff is in the key of F#, here open A and E major chords are predominant – those with the most amount of reverberation on a conventionally tuned guitar. This noise, accompanied by screams, gives added weight to John's closing words, 'I wanna be free', to which several commentators have attached great significance, even implying they were an ad lib. However, less prominent on the Barrett Strong original, this line does appear on its fade-out.

When John identified *With the Beatles* as the album he would most like to re-mix, he probably had this track in his thoughts. Often overriding George Martin's better judgement, the group piled overdub upon overdub to build up a sound that could replicate the echo and atmosphere of the Cavern or the Star Club. This was in vain, as two-track recording machines could only take limited amounts of over-dubbing before distorting. In particular, the backing vocals end up with a blurred tone.

MR MOONLIGHT
Written by Roy Lee Johnson
A recording on 14th August 1964 was rejected and re-made in four takes on 18th October
Found on *Beatles For Sale*

Hearing John record his soaring lead vocal, studio engineer, Geoff Emerick, recalled the hairs rising on the back of his neck. John's plea to the night sky, as if sung by some Spanish street singer, is thrilling even if the same could not be said of the corny verses. Originally the B-side of an obscure 1962 single by Dr Feelgood and the Interns, it was most likely available to the Beatles through the large catalogue of records held at Brian Epstein's store in Liverpool. They spotted the muted performance with its strained vocals could be bettered and that its histrionics allowed a rare chance for dramatisation. So George comically thwacks an African drum to announce the start of each chorus and Paul improvised a kitsch Hammond organ solo.

MOTHER NATURE'S SON
McCartney
John, George and Ringo do not play on this track

Basic track recorded 9th August 1968, overdubs on 20th August
Found on *The Beatles* aka The White Album

Only once we truly feel ourselves at one with nature, through methods such as meditation, can we realise our full consciousness and health: this was the message the Beatles received from the Maharishi Mahesh Yogi, who extolled what he called natural law. After a suitably humbling and persuasive lecture on this subject in India, both John and Paul put these thoughts into lyrics. Paul created 'Mother Nature's Son' while John wrote 'Child of Nature' which later evolved into 'Jealous Guy'. For two such forceful individuals, both songs employ unusually subdued melodies and words. Paul paints a humble picture of his youth, with a small melancholy grouping of trumpets and trombones evoking a romantic vision of the Lancashire countryside. Unlike the typical Lennon/McCartney lyric, the listener is not invited in – the streams and the fields are a private setting for reflection. It as if the Maharishi had shrunk Paul's ego and he is dwarfed by nature; the mountain, the stream, even the swinging daisies he sings of tower over him and his spindly guitar.

THE NIGHT BEFORE
McCartney
John plays keyboard for the first time on a Beatles' track
Recorded in two takes on 17th February 1965
Found on *Help!*

Paul's account of being given the cold shoulder after a one night stand is hard to believe. Given his status as a pop prince, the rude awakening is far more likely to be for the girl he meets. It makes better sense seen as an attempt to emulate Bob Dylan's 'I Don't Believe You (She Acts like We Have Never Met)' from *Another Side of Bob Dylan* – an account of a night of passion with an unnamed woman, who then disowns him. John's 'You've Got to Hide Your Love Away' takes a line from the tale too, and it seems likely that over the break at the start of 1965 both John and Paul had competitively set out to emulate Dylan. Though where John's tale is mournful, Paul's is bright, which serves to make his message of woe less credible. Whilst it shines for its infectious harmonies and syncopated mix of guitar and Hammond organ, the pop world was becoming more cerebral and Paul appears out of sync.

NO REPLY
Music: Lennon/McCartney Words: Lennon
Recorded in eight takes on 30th September 1964
Found on *Beatles For Sale*

A work in progress from the end of the *A Hard Day's Night* sessions until the start of *Beatles for Sale*, the extra thought led to a string of tricks to bring alive its tale of infidelity. It was given a flamenco theme with acoustic guitar flecks, double-time handclaps and alliteration of certain words ('tried to telephone') which mimic the effect of castanets. The twists in the tale are backed by sudden mood changes. The switch from the investigation into his girlfriend's infidelity to an admonishment of the error of her ways is emphasised with group handclaps, Paul following John's vocal and George Martin on piano. All strongly hint at the support John has for his case against his girlfriend. But there is no happy ending. Alone, his voice concludes with a single resonant piano chord.

The story was inspired by 'Silhouettes', a US hit for the Rays in 1957 which was later covered by Herman's Hermits, in which the singer believes he sees his lover embracing another man in a window. Unlike the gloom of 'No Reply', there is a twist to the Ray's tale. When the singer knocks on the door, he finds he has called at the wrong house. Curiously, 'No Reply' at times reads like a picture story from a girl's comic, a purpose for which several Lennon/McCartney songs had already been adapted in 1964.

NORWEGIAN WOOD (This Bird Has Flown)

Words: John/ Paul   Music: John/ Paul
Written in February 1965, Paul helped write the middle eight and the closing lines.
After a first attempt on 12th October 1965, it was remade on 21st October
Found on *Rubber Soul*

A pastiche that transcends its source, John's tale of a bohemian encounter with a mystery woman echoes the relationship songs on *Another Side Of Bob Dylan*. Notably, where the opening line to 'Ballad In Plain D' starts by telling us how Dylan 'once' loved a girl, here John's gambit is to tell us how he 'once' met a girl. Similarly, the enigmatic use of parentheses in the title, follows 'I Don't Believe You (She Acts Like We Have Never Met)'.

But John goes further. Where Dylan deals in code and private imagery over lengthy and numerous verses, John tells it succinctly. And where Dylan's recordings were roughly finished, here there is a broad wash of acoustic guitars. Also, instead of harmonica, a sitar helps conjure up the exotic central character and the bohemian setting of the flat where John finds himself.

There has been much guesswork as to whom John was writing about, but it is safest to stick to his explanation of it being a composite of different women he'd had affairs with behind his wife's back. He felt a growing frustration with his wife, who embraced domesticity whilst he sought out new experiences. His tastes led him to seek the company of women who were sophisticated, worldly and artistic, and often older than himself. Indeed, John hints that it is the woman who takes the lead in meeting and seducing him. Still nervous of giving too much away, he dissembles. The cute anecdote about sleeping in the bath avoids suggesting sex took place, but an early demo is more suggestive. On the *Anthology 2* version he sings of how he once 'had' a girl, but on the final mix he double tracks this with 'met'.

Using Dylan's method of writing the words first and then fitting a tune to it, his melody echoes the jaunty structure of folk songs such as 'Scarborough Fair'. Ostensibly his most mature song so far, it contains a hidden joke as if John and Paul had become self-conscious of how serious they had become. The conclusion, dreamt up by Paul, was that John should light a fire, not so much one in a grate, but to the apartment itself.

NOT A SECOND TIME

Lennon
Recorded in nine takes on 11th September 1963
Found on *With the Beatles*

Superficially simple, 'Not A Second Time' invites investigation for the way it uncannily echoes the themes of John's later works. Its basic message 'you left me and hurt me, but now you've come back, I don't want or trust you anymore' precedes the abandonment anxiety of 'Don't Let Me Down', 'Jealous Guy' and 'I'm Losing You'. Such anxiety is attributed to his loss of contact with his parents at the age of five. Indeed 'Not a Second Time' uncannily echoes the sentiment of his 1970 recording 'Mother', on which he tackles his parents 'betrayal' head on. If such demons were at the heart of the words, the music bears little relation. Its mood is happy, from George Martin's tea dance solo, to a beat which owes something to the Miracles rave-up 'Mickey's Monkey'. If anything, it reflects the

Beatles' joy at making music and the lesser priority they gave in 1963-64 of matching lyrics to mood.

NOWHERE MAN

Lennon
Paul speculated this was in part about the state of John's marriage
Recordings made on 20th October 1965 were scrapped and remade the following day
Found on *Rubber Soul*

There can be little doubt as to whom John based this character on, even though it is sung in the third person. It voiced fears over his future, after he had quickly achieved all his early ambitions for fame and fortune. 'Nowhere' referred to the grand private estate where he lived in a 20-roomed mansion overlooking a golf course, spending days cut off from the outside world. Soon after writing 'Nowhere Man', he told the journalist, Maureen Cleave, he was keen to move on, as the estate was primarily for stock-brokers who thought it "really was the end".

Undoubtedly influenced by 'Like a Rolling Stone', which was in the charts during its recording, Bob Dylan's protagonist has also ended up somewhere he had not intended. Dylan's character is partly autobiographical, too, drawing on his own experiences of turning up homeless and unknown in New York as a teenager. However, unlike Dylan's often coded and surreal verses, 'Nowhere Man' is a model of plain and direct language. Unlike the first person plea for attention of 'Help!', this is a character who could be 'you' or 'me'. It encourages the listener to imagine themselves not only with the same insecurities, but also with the same solution, which is effectively 'don't worry, be happy'.

Recalling the creation of 'Nowhere Man' John said he spent five hours one night trying to write something "meaningful and good". Giving up, he lay down defeated, at which point, to his relief and amazement, the lyrics occurred to him on the spot. His elation at this is clear in one of his most uplifting melodies.

OB-LA-DI, OB-LA-DA

McCartney

The song has its roots in four different continents. It was written in India, recorded in London, inspired by Caribbean music while its title is taken from a Nigerian phrase meaning 'life goes on'.

Recordings made on 3rd, 4th and 5th July 1968 were rejected. A finished take was recorded on 8th July, though a remake was attempted on 9th July. Overdubs were added on 9th, 11th, 12th and 15th July

Found on *The Beatles* aka The White Album

A byword for inter-band bickering and musical differences, 'Ob-la-di, Ob-la-da's five through-the-night recordings sessions pushed band comradeship to breaking point. As a fan of ska, John was at first enthusiastic, but then worn down by trying to perfect an unfamiliar rhythm long into the night. Arguments soon began to break out and accounts attest to how, on the fourth night, John stormed in and announced he had a new piano riff for the intro and they should record it there and then. This proved to be the final take, though Paul tested everyone's patience with another try-out a day later.

In what can only be seen as revenge, John and George vetoed any suggestion it should become a single. Neither could have relished the prospect of promoting on TV what they saw as a childish song, indeed George later name-checked it on 'Savoy Truffle', his skit on the contents of a sickly-sweet box of chocolates. Chastened by the rejection, Paul responded by introducing the heavy rocker 'Helter Skelter' a week later.

Paul's loss was to the gain of Scottish group, Marmalade, who had a UK No.1 with 'Ob-la-di Ob-la-da' in January 1969. On the verge of being dropped by their record label, they celebrated their first hit by wearing kilts to promote it on TV.

Paul's inspiration came from Jimmy Scott and the Obla-di Obla-da band, a London-based ska group whom he had seen live on several occasions. Scott asked for financial recompense after hearing of the track and Paul acknowledged this in an unusual way. Sentenced to a three-month stretch in Brixton prison for non-payment of alimony, Scott was released after Beatles' fixer, Alistair Taylor, went to the prison to pay off the outstanding money, apparently £800 in total.

OCTOPUS'S GARDEN
Words: Starkey   Music: Starkey/Harrison
Basic track recorded 26th April 1969 with overdubs on 29th April, 17th and 18th July
Found on *Abbey Road*

Ringo had a barrage of awkward questions to face after he had left the world's most popular group with half an album to finish in August 1968. Frustration at Paul's perfectionist demands and the general level of group bickering had tested the limits of his patience. Fleeing the country, he put himself out of contact of telephones or telegrams on a Mediterranean sea cruise. There the boat's captain told him of the lives of octopuses and how they built gardens of stones on the sea floor. This struck a chord with him because, as he recalled, this was exactly where he felt like being. It is a mark of his anguish that he describes life under the sea as a hideaway, the same word Paul uses in his hymn to regret, 'Yesterday'. He also refers to the reasons for the split, by imagining an octopus's life as one free from being told what to do.

After a short hiatus where the remaining Beatles worked with Paul on drums, a telegram from them eventually reached Ringo with the message that he was the greatest drummer in the world and asking him to return which he duly did (Ringo's walk-out spanned 22nd August – 3rd September 1968). Their desire to bury the hatchet led to a sweetening of Ringo's moment of anguish some months later, George playing a big role in this. The *Let It Be* film shows Ringo had written only a basic verse or two and was seeking George's help in completing it. As George later co-wrote and produced several of Ringo's singles and plays the intricate surf guitar intro, it seems fair to award him a writing credit.

OH! DARLING

McCartney
The vocal harmonies here were the last contribution John made to the Beatles on 11th August 1969
Basic track recorded 20th April 1969, overdubs 26th April, 17th,18th, 22nd, 23rd July, 8th, 11th August
Found on *Abbey Road*

Combine the exaggerated emotions here with the hip-nonsense verse of 'Come Together' and you have the genesis of glam rock, a music steeped in Fifties' rock'n'roll but without the innocence. Paul is all mock pathos and melodrama, pleading that he will fall down and die if his 'darling' leaves, beseeching us to believe this statement is true – the overdriven guitars matching his exaggeration. Before recording he spent days roughening his voice for impact, but John, who plays piano here, claimed he could have still sung it better. In the context of his obsessive relationship with Yoko, perhaps he would have sung it straight.

OLD BROWN SHOE

Harrison
B-side of 'Ballad of John and Yoko'
Basic track recorded 16th April 1969, overdubs 18th April
Found on *Past Masters*

George clearly had something to be happy about when he made 'Old Brown Shoe' but it is hard to know what. Possibly it was the return of sun and warmth which also inspired 'Here Comes The Sun' in April 1969. It is broadly about discovering a new lease of life – its title could equally be 'Stepping Out' – but the only hint at what is causing this carefree spirit is the reference to escaping 'this zoo'. Plausibly, this could have been relief at the end of the *Let It Be* project weeks before, where he had been under the constant scrutiny of film cameras. The music expresses his new zeal, with leaping bass lines and sharp tempo changes.

ONE AFTER 909

Lennon/McCartney
Recorded live on Savile Row rooftop, London 30th January 1969
Found on *Anthology 1* and *Let It Be*

The small repertoire and limited abilities of John and Paul's first band, the Quarrymen, meant their first songs laid bare their influences. The rhythm of the verses on 'One After 909' is reminiscent of Jerry Lee Lewis's 'Whole Lotta Shakin' Goin' On' and the chorus is similar to the stuttered tempo of 'Great Balls of Fire'. The lyrics echo the international skiffle hit 'Freight Train'. Where Nancy Whiskey sang of seeking to leave on train 'old number nine' but asks the listener not to tell anyone else, here 'One After 909' reads as if written by her lover, describing a run to the station to stop his 'baby' from leaving. Resurrected at the end of the Beatles' career to symbolise a return to their roots, their inability to take it seriously showed why this could never truly happen. The clumsy structure and naive, innocent words were only a reminder of how far they had moved on.

ONLY A NORTHERN SONG

George Harrison
"A joke", George '80
Northern Songs was the name of the Beatles' publishing company,
only 49% of which was owned by the group.
Basic track recorded 13th February 1967, overdubs 14th February and
20th April
Found on *Yellow Submarine*

George wrote this during the four days he idly watched
John and Paul put 'A Day in the Life' together. His input
was barely needed. He had been given the humiliating role
of playing maracas, but was then demoted to bongos after
he was judged to be not keeping time. It is easy to picture
him sitting seething on the side-lines while he wrote this
verse to stave off his boredom at watching Paul conduct
the cacophonous orchestral crescendo. He duly describes
feeling as if he was 'not there', as well as feeling 'not right'.
There is a parallel to the contemporary hit, 'They're
Coming To Take Me Away Ha-Ha', by Napoleon XIV.
An unhinged lyric set to discordant music, it is a tale of
how after being left by a partner, the singer has gone mad
and is being sent to the 'funny farm'. George in his own
way seems to be letting off steam at how John and Paul
were affecting his mental health or at the very least how
useless they were making him feel. As part of his protest
the most prominent instruments on 'Only A Northern
Song' are played by the two members of the group who
were most marginalised during the making of *Sgt.Pepper's*
– George on organ and Ringo on drums. George later
called the song a 'joke', but to Paul it must have come as a
slight as it was rejected from *Sgt.Pepper's*. As if to
underline this, the discordant trumpet and glockenspiel
were added after recording had ended for *Sgt.Pepper's*,
perhaps to underline that it was now only truly fit for the
Yellow Submarine cartoon.

PAPERBACK WRITER

Words: McCartney Music: McCartney/Lennon
Single first released 30th May 1966
Basic track recorded on 13th April 1966 overdubs 14th April
Found on *Past Masters*

Could a two-chord song with previously-unheard levels
of guitar distortion reach the top of the charts? This was
the exciting challenge the Beatles set themselves when
creating the dynamic, hook-laden 'Paperback Writer'.

Compressors installed at Abbey Road studios in early
1966 permitted microphones to record higher volume.
Amplifier distortion could now be put on tape in a
controlled fashion and the low tones of the bass were given
the same attack as six-string guitars. As such, the opening
riff was not subtle, but it must have felt amazing to put such
sound onto disc. Further in, the textures of the distorted
guitars make their notes blend in original ways. That Paul
credited John with helping him on the music, rather than
his usual role of lyric doctor, shows how excited they both
were at this new freedom. Credit should also be given to
their bold new chief engineer Geoff Emerick too.

For good measure the group took another step in the
dark by dropping the 'you', 'me', 'love' formulas of their
previous singles and by singing of a fictional character.
Change was a matter of urgency. The Beatles were in the
unusual position of playing catch-up on three singles
released in March 1966 which pushed pop into noisy and
extreme directions. The Byrds layered a mesh of distorted
rhythm guitars on 'Eight Miles High', while distortion
featured prominently on the Yardbirds' 'Shapes of Things'.
The monotonal anti-love song 'Substitute' by The Who,
also holds a single chord over long stretches and features
hyper-active drumming. 'Paperback Writer' not only
matches these but is smarter. Its use of a French nursery
rhyme, 'Frère Jacques', sung as a harmony vocal gives a
mocking contrast to the music's bombast.

This experiment, if a personal thrill for the group, was less favoured by the public, for whilst still a No.1 in the US and the UK it was one of their lowest-selling singles, sustaining only one week at the top in the US before being replaced by Frank Sinatra's 'Strangers In The Night'.

PENNY LANE

Words: McCartney/ Lennon   Music: McCartney
Double A-side with 'Strawberry Fields Forever' first released 13th February 1967
At five verses, this is the longest lyric Paul wrote with the Beatles. The verses contain several pieces of smut – a finger pie and the rhyming of 'Queen' with an analogy for a penis ('clean machine'). The making of 'Penny Lane' logged up 54 hours in the studio. This is the longest taken on a Beatles' song and is more than it took to complete their first two albums. A basic piano track was recorded on 29th December 1966 and piece-meal all other parts were added on 30th December, 4th, 5th, 6th 9th, 10th, 12th and 17th January 1967
Found on *Magical Mystery Tour*

What John and Paul valued about their childhood years in Liverpool is summed up in two songs written within weeks of each other. 'Penny Lane' is a paean to a junction of suburban roads with a bus shelter and shops where ordinary people congregated and went about their everyday lives, whilst 'Strawberry Fields Forever' tells of an escape into a fantastical mini-kingdom created in a remote over-grown walled garden. Where John sought unheralded levels of sound manipulation to convey this lost world, Paul sought a clean touch with tones as wholesome and varied as the characters he paints. To do this on four recording tracks without loss of sound quality meant a production line of musicians queuing up for a brief moment on one of the precious tracks. First, flutes play staccato notes, a piccolo (similar to a flute) plays a harmony, then trumpets and flugelhorn enter on the chorus. A few notes of oboe and then a piccolo trumpet solo enter half-way through and from here, in a gradual crescendo, the brass takes the place of the flutes, before all return for a final fanfare. This is topped off with David Mason's extraordinary piccolo trumpet solo – a late addition to the mix. Paul, had seen a version of Bach's 2nd Brandenburg Concerto played on TV, where Mason played the main melody, unlike the decorative role he plays here and realised this was the missing element he needed and duly instructed George Martin to make it happen. (The Cor Anglais, a double reed oboe, which is listed among the instruments for 'Penny Lane' appears to have been discarded as a result).

In the longest amount of studio time devoted to a single Beatles' song – much of it spent layering piano overdubs – an array of sound effects was added too. John sings the odd word of the lead vocals, notably 'summer' at 1.39 – possibly a low note Paul could not adequately reach, a few notes of double bass appear at 2.05, then there is the ringing of a bell and a crack of thunder. The attention to detail, the high fidelity and the glorious harmonies show that whilst not a love song per se, it has a claim to being Paul's most heartfelt creation.

PIGGIES

Words: Harrison/Lennon Music: Harrison
Recorded 19th and 20th September 1968
Found on *The Beatles* aka The White Album

Anyone with great influence over the behaviour of young people should be mindful of their public utterances. This was a responsibility the Beatles bore heavier than others due to their international fame, but in the toxic atmosphere of the *White Album* sessions, it was harder to maintain. Not only did this vicious satire of the English upper classes sneak through, but there was also anger at the rich American who goes off to India to shoot tigers on

'Bungalow Bill', and the eulogising of a psychopath on 'Maxwell's Silver Hammer' which was written at the album's close. At the heart of each, was a desire to amuse as much as to shock and the use of chamber orchestra instruments, harpsichord and strings, made George's satire come alive. Tragically, the lyrics to 'Piggies' ended up as a part of the twisted visions of the psychopath, Charles Manson. His gang knifed six people to death in the affluent suburb of Benedict Canyon, Los Angeles, in August 1969, with one of the victim's blood being used to write the word 'piggies' on the wall. While George had to suffer the opprobrium, ironically its most damaging lines were from his mother, who suggested the need for the piggies to receive a 'whacking', while John contributed the cannibalistic line about using knives and forks to eat bacon.

PLEASE MR POSTMAN

Written by Garrett/Bateman/Dobbins/Holland/Gorman
'Deliver de letter, the sooner le bet,' John mucks up the lyrics at 2.12
Recorded in nine takes on 30th July 1963
Found on *With The Beatles*

An appetite for loud, hard-driven rock in Hamburg encouraged an extreme dramatisation of cover versions. John was happy to oblige with frenzied takes of otherwise plaintive US hits. So, whereas Gladys Horton sounds forlorn at the postman passing her by again on the Marvelettes' 'Please Mr Postman', John sings it as if fleeing a fire. The popularity of his version has made it pre-eminent, so where Horton sings of it being a 'mighty long time', most others now sing it as a 'long, long time'. Unlike the original, John's voice is double-tracked for greater intensity at the loss of intimacy. George Martin objected but was over-ruled – indeed John later regretted this, recalling *With The Beatles* he said: "we double-tracked ourselves off the album".

'Please Mr Postman' was the Motown label's first US No.1 and featured a pre-fame Marvin Gaye on drums. Its lyrics were written by the Marvelettes' singer, Georgia Dobbins, who has since contested the way it was attributed to five writers. She claimed the only other credit belonged to William Garrett who added the tune.

PLEASE PLEASE ME (album)
Recorded in 18.15 hours and mixed in six hours
Ten tracks were recorded on 11th February 1963 (four tracks recorded in 1962)
Album released 22nd March 1963

The Beatles' debut album follows a blueprint from an artist they professed to dislike. *Cliff* was created in the very same No. 2 studio at Abbey Road, four years earlier, almost to the day. Cliff Richard's debut was recorded in front of a small group of fans to capture the excitement of his live act on 10th February 1959 and became the biggest-selling UK album of that year.

George Martin, who shared the use of the studio with Cliff's producer, Norrie Paramour, would have been well aware of this precedent. In a quote he gave to Mersey Beat newspaper on 26th November 1962, he talked of plans to record the album live. Knowing of the group's popularity at the Cavern, he suggested it might be made there or as a show in front of a small group of fans at Abbey Road. After visiting the Cavern, Martin ruled it out as too damp and chaotic and plumped for a quick one-off live recording of 10 songs, without audience, on a spare day in the middle of the group's first UK tour. The rush came from the need to have an album to cash-in on the success of the single 'Please Please Me' which was then riding high in the charts. There are minimal overdubs and amplifiers were faced to the walls to re-create the reverberation one would hear at the Cavern. The only lack of verity was the failure of

Martin and his engineer, Norman Smith, to capture the raucous attack of the group's guitars heard on the Hamburg tapes from six weeks before. However, the music did toughen over the course of the day and the vocals became more passionate. This can be heard in the order of recording: 'There's a Place', 'I Saw Her Standing There', 'Hold Me Tight' (rejected and re-recorded for *With The Beatles*), 'A Taste of Honey', 'Do You Want To Know a Secret?', 'Misery', 'Anna', 'Boys', 'Chains', 'Baby It's You' and finally, 'Twist And Shout'. The song list is revealing of the way the group still saw themselves as a professional club band, by including current chart hits, the Cookies 'Chains' and Acker Bilk's 'A Taste of Honey'.

POLYTHENE PAM (See page 177)

PLEASE PLEASE ME
Lennon/McCartney
Single released 11th January 1963
Recorded in 18 takes on 26th November 1962
Found on *Please Please Me*

The presence of this piece of smut so early in the Beatles' career is so shocking to most it has been largely ignored. While John wrote many true love songs with Paul early on, when left to his own devices he tended to need a bold or cheeky spin for inspiration. And when sitting down in his bedroom in Liverpool for a single in the summer of 1962 he would have been well aware of Mike Sarne's novelty hit 'Come Outside', which was the UK's No.1 from the end of June to the beginning of July. A comic tale of a man trying to make a woman more amorous with him, it features the repeated exhortation to 'come outside'. John's request was also full of sexual innuendo and features the repeated cry 'come on'. Such smut survived owing to the lack of open discussion of sex in this era and the low likelihood of anyone drawing attention to it. Oddly, John never spoke of this openly and it fell to Paul, in an interview with the Observer in 1967, to admit there was a double-entendre. In this early guise it mimicked the slow pace of Roy Orbison's 'Only the Lonely' – the idea of Orbison singing such risqué lyrics must have been part of the joke. Almost certainly unaware of the connotations, George Martin only objected to its tempo and asked for it to be speeded up. The group followed this advice with gusto, the final recording being two minutes of cascading noise and adrenalin capturing the raw thrill of their live shows. In a complex arrangement it packs in three separate riffs – the opening harmonica, the chiming lead guitar and the accelerating rhythm guitar. It also finds time to stop for a drum-fill and at the end, as if out of bravado, a coolly-executed cadence, where John holds a single note as the guitars descend in key and tempo to a final chord. Showing that this exuberance is for real, you can clearly hear John pause to catch his breath at 1.02.

The thrill transferred so well to disc that Dick James, the group's new publisher, secured them an immediate booking on the UK national TV show, *Thank Your Lucky Stars*, simply by playing it over the phone to the show's producer.

PS I LOVE YOU

McCartney
B-side to 'Love Me Do'
Session musician, Andy White, plays drums, Ringo plays maracas.
Recorded in 10 takes on 11th September 1962
Found on *Please Please Me*

Polite requests and endearments were the formula for the first three Beatles' singles. Keen to make the best first impression on their record company and the public they hid their boisterousness behind polite phrases: 'love me do', 'PS, I love you',' please, please me', 'ask me why', 'from me to you' and 'thank you, girl'. They also felt the need to demonstrate they were more than the average rock 'n' roll band. The cha-cha beat here matches the Latin rhythms which made 'Rock-a-Hula-Baby' by Elvis Presley one of the biggest British hits of the year, while for good measure Paul's deep-toned lead vocal seeks out the baritone of his hero.

Written in Hamburg in response to Brian Epstein's request for new material for EMI, its first line could be read as a longing to get back to England to meet this challenge. Indeed, in his biography, Paul had no qualms in dashing the popularly-held notion that it was about the letters he wrote to his girlfriend, Dot Rhone, in Liverpool.

RAIN
Words: Lennon   Music: Lennon/ McCartney
B-side to 'Paperback Writer'
The basic track was recorded on 14th April 1966 overdubs on 16th April
Found on *Past Masters*

Both simple and complicated this is both about the mundane nature of weather and a state of higher consciousness. Grounded in the simplicity of steady strokes of the chords G, C and D on guitar, but giving licence for cascading drums fills and wild bass runs, the hip superiority of the words and the sneering tone in the vocals tell of the insight John has had into life, but which others have failed to get. It tells of his holiday in Tahiti and an arrival on tour in Melbourne where he experienced monsoon rainfall of the like unseen in England: by this benchmark the English weather must have seemed trivial. It also serves as an analogy for the small in-group of society who had tried the drug LSD. It is a more persuasive message than the bad acid trip of 'Tomorrow Never

Knows'. Rather than telling us to switch off our minds, here he seductively tells us that the everyday hang-ups we have (for the British this is the eternal moan about rainy weather) can be overcome if we live more like him. These altered states are hinted at by having the guitar and vocals recorded fast and then slowed down on tape to give them a synthetic texture. This and the closing backwards vocals made 'Rain' as much an exciting first in recorded sound as 'Paperback Writer' and both were released on single two months ahead of *Revolver*, to give another first over their rivals. For posterity though, 'Rain' would be better served by being on *Revolver* where it is arguably superior to John's other compositions.

Rejected songs

Songs written and recorded by the Beatles, but given no official release during the band's lifetime
First released 1995-96
Found on Anthology I, II and III

Surely the most unloved Lennon/McCartney reject is 'If You've Got Trouble'. It was not only passed on by Ringo but lacks any credible cover version. An unconvincing step into put-down lyrics aimed at a spoilt, emotionally demanding, diamond-wearing girl, it has an uncanny parallel with the Rolling Stones' 'Play with Fire' recorded only weeks before in early 1965. Both tackle class antagonism and end with the threat that unless the girl's behaviour changes she should return to her rich idyll. The Stones were more at home with severity and the suspicion must be that Ringo was being used to test it out. Ill at ease with his band-mates' experiment and an oafish arrangement, he sabotaged the only take.

Another failed experiment on Help was 'That Means A Lot', a passionate, if muddled, piece of philosophy on those who are cynical about love. It can be read as a prototype of the positive thinking of 'We Can Work It Out' and 'Hey Jude', but here Paul's banal message is only that a love has meaning for him, but not for another.

From the same year the wooden '12 Bar Original' is more worthy of a second-rate garage band. Commonly seen as an easy fix to fill Rubber Soul *to deadline, it may just have been an experimental jam session never intended to be preserved on tape.*

There are several compositions by George which suffered by being shut out of the Lennon/McCartney partnership. His promising if slight 'You Know What To Do' from the A Hard Day's Night sessions is crying out for a middle eight, a lyrical twist or harmony from his band-mates. He grew bitter at this neglect and 'Not Guilty' from 1968 unleashes some of this resentment to no effect.

'REVOLUTION 1' & 'REVOLUTION'

Lennon
'Revolution' was B-side to 'Hey Jude' released 1968
The melody is similar to 'The Old Man and the Mule' by James Ray from 1962.
The basic track for 'Revolution 1' was recorded on 30th May 1968 with overdubs on 31st May, 4th June and 21st June.
A rehearsal of 'Revolution' was made on 9th July 1968 at Abbey Road, a backing track was recorded on 10th July and overdubs added on 11th and 12th July
Found on *The Beatles* aka The White Album and *Past Masters*

A pop act with a chart hit entitled 'Revolution' would have generated great publicity in the 1960s. This had been John's intention when he sought a quick release in response to the barricades erected in Paris in May 1968. "I wanted it out as a single, as a statement of the Beatles' position on Vietnam and the Beatles' position on revolution", he recalled. The impact as the A-side of a single would have been incendiary. In its first recording ('Revolution 1') John asks to be counted 'out'/'in' of any revolution, while this is confusing, simply the suggestion of the Beatles wanting to be 'counted in' could have led it to being banned over fears of it inciting unrest. Such concerns surely led to Paul and George to veto it as an A-side although they voiced their opposition in terms of its slow pace and therefore the likelihood of it not selling much. John's frustration was great. He had written it in March and April, a month before the unrest in Paris made world headlines. This prescience must have convinced him of its worth and of its importance over any assessment of musical strength. Indeed, its recording was not to their usual standards. Seeking to rely on George Martin less, John took the lead on the orchestration of brass. However, he confusingly he gave his powerful message a sleepy arrangement, in an apparent sarcastic contrast*. Taking the group's criticism to heart he sought a faster more emphatic heavy rock remake two weeks later. Here, he clearly asked to be counted 'out' of any revolution and to make this extra clear key words are double-tracked. This was a big improvement on the track finished in June, but all talk of it being made an A-side was over when 'Hey Jude' was created weeks later.

However wise the message has proved in hindsight, its pacifism was unpopular with those students and intellectuals radicalised by opposition to the Vietnam war. They felt Western societies were on the verge of major change, in which they wanted the Beatles to assist. The criticism made John doubt his words and, by way of redress on 'Power To The People' in 1971, he sang that those seeking a revolution should go out and get it.

*Possibly he was thinking of the doo-wop spoofs of the Mothers of Invention, in particular, 'What's The Ugliest Part of Your Body?' The answer to lead singer Frank Zappa's question was not the subject's nose or toes, as the words tell, but their 'mind'. John, too, not only warns us of hateful minds but also urges us to free our minds.

John Lennon's Revolution

John was carrying out his own personal revolution in the spring and summer of 1968 inspired in part by the rebellion in Paris. He had first walked out on the Maharishi and renounced his faith in his teachings. Then he sought to end a marriage that had cramped his style for six years – on the flight back from India he ungraciously told his wife of every woman he had slept with during their marriage. Weeks later, he moved in with Yoko Ono, who, in a breach of band convention, he now brought to all recording sessions. In the studio he developed an aggressive attitude to his band-mates, the engineers and to George Martin too. Much of this was done to re-establish his leadership and to rest the artistic direction of the group back off Paul. The one revolution he was not yet ready for was the break-up of the Beatles, which would follow a year later.

REVOLUTION 9

Lennon/Ono
At 8 minutes and 22 seconds this is the longest Beatles' track.
Created at home with Yoko Ono and at Abbey Road studios
Recorded and edited 10th, 11th, 20th and 25th June 1968
Found on *The Beatles* aka The White Album

This was the first tuneless jumble of disembodied words and sound effects to be commercially released by a band best known for sweet, melodic pop songs. The disgust and astonishment it produced must have appealed to John's love of shocking others and follows in the line of stunts such as peeing out of a window in sight of church-goers in Hamburg.

The unpopularity of 'Revolution 9' lies in our inability to detect any skill or artistry over its eight minutes and any kudos it has gained since is for the sheer bravado of the Beatles in releasing it.

John grandly described it as an 'unconscious picture' of revolution, which reveals how frightening he found the prospect: its disembodied, emotionless voices and anarchic sound are the stuff of nightmare. Later, when talking to the left-wing newspaper, Red Mole, and trying to maintain his man of the people credentials he referred to its mood as a mistake.

REVOLVER
Recorded in 216 hours and mixed in 48 hours
Album released August 5th 1966

The name *Revolver* is a play on words, being both the action of a record on a turntable and a weapon. Metaphorically, it was a record to shoot down the group's rivals who had threatened to eclipse them with a string of bold records in the winter of 1965/66. The Who's 'My Generation' had broadcast the shocking line that the lead singer hoped he died before he got old. Mick Jagger proclaimed that when he looked inside himself his heart was 'black' on 'Paint It Black', while the Shangri-La's hit 'Leader of the Pack' was a paean to a dead biker whose fatal road crash is recreated on record.

Revolver responded with 'She Said She Said' which spoke of knowing what it was like to be dead and with 'Eleanor Rigby' which alludes to the digging of a grave for its main character and even confronts us with detail such as the dirt on the hands of the grave digger.

References to drugs were also now *de rigeur*. While the damage inflicted by illicit drugs are common knowledge today, in the mid-sixties, drugs such as marijuana and LSD were seen as a liberation from a society that was resistant to new ideas or differences. Bob Dylan's 'Rainy Day Women # 12 & 35' sang of getting 'stoned', the Rolling Stones' '19th Nervous Breakdown' alluded to taking LSD, 'Mothers' Little Helper' sang of a yellow pill (a Nembutal). 'Yellow Submarine', a track popularly seen to refer to the nickname for a Nembutal followed soon after.   'Dr

Robert', 'Got To Get You Into My Life' and 'Tomorrow Never Knows', refer to drugs, whilst 'Rain' and 'She Said, She Said' were inspired by experiences whilst on LSD.

Bolder words demanded music to match and discord was used to convey this. The duelling discordant guitars on the Byrds 'Eight Miles High' sought to mimic the sound of a sitar, an effect which is reproduced on 'And Your Bird Can Sing', 'Rain' and 'She Said, She Said'. Long mono-chordal sections, similar to their use in Indian music were used on 'Eleanor Rigby', 'Got To Get You Into My Life', 'Love You Too', 'Paperback Writer' and 'Tomorrow Never Knows'.

However, everything on *Revolver* is clearer and more powerful than anything it was inspired by, not least because it took advantage of new technology. Artificial double-tracking meant a vocal, once on tape, could be fed back a second time, at a fraction of a second's difference, giving a slicker more accurate sound. Improved compressors and limiters allowed tape to capture the loudness of amplifier distortion and for bass guitar to be louder on vinyl.

These innovations were imperative. The group had a fiery meeting prior to recording where they demanded a quality of sound equal to the records they were hearing from US studios. Geoff Emerick, the group's new chief engineer, recalled John and Paul threatening to record elsewhere. In a measure of how far EMI not only responded to these demands but exceeded them, Paul later boasted to the press: "They are sounds that nobody else has done yet. I mean nobody *ever.*"

Revolver benefited from a three months lay off at the beginning of 1966. Paul used the time to see a string of bands, operas, plays and exhibitions and was quoted in the New Musical Express saying: "I've stopped thinking anything is weird or different". The quote could have easily come from John, who retreated to his mansion indulging in a destructive, if occasionally revelatory, exploration of his psyche through LSD as well as ploughing through numerous books.

ROCK 'N' ROLL MUSIC
Written by Chuck Berry
Recorded in one take on 18th October 1964
Found on *Beatles For Sale*

When Chuck Berry put himself in character as a teenager singing about his love of rock 'n' roll, he sang it with all the wry observation of a 31 year-old. By contrast, a 23 year-old John sings it as the teenager he was when he first heard it. Indeed, he cranks up the energy levels so high he misses Berry's intended humour. Berry did not hate jazz, but John did – so where the lyrics say that if played too fast it 'changes' the beauty of its melody, he sings this as 'loses'. The piano, too, follows the chords for heavy impact, unlike on the original where it plays decorative notes, not dissimilar, ironically to jazz. John's passion caused him to fluff the words. On a busy day in the studio he mis-sings 'oughta got rock 'n' roll music' at 2.19.

ROCKY RACOON
McCartney
Recorded in nine takes on 15th August 1968
Some of the lyrics were written on the spot in the studio
Found on *The Beatles* aka The White Album

John and Paul entertained themselves and the American guests at the Maharishi's meditation camp in India with story songs. To cater for their audience, 'Rocky Racoon' was made in a cod Country and Western style, while John's 'Bungalow Bill' alluded to the anti-Vietnam war chants aimed at US president, Lyndon Johnson. Paul wins out for his arrangement – getting the Beatles to play like a hokey Wild West saloon bar band is far more amusing than the massed acoustic guitars of 'Bungalow Bill'. Recorded live, John's harmonica playing and bass and George Martin's piano are particularly believable. Paul, though, loses out for lyrical impact; his tale might have won him a few laughs on its first rendition in India, but it is essentially a shaggy dog story. For John, the thrill was airing sharp social messages, indeed Paul recognised this too, citing 'Bungalow Bill' as one of the first-ever animal rights songs.

ROLL OVER BEETHOVEN
Written by Chuck Berry
Recorded in eight takes on 30th July 1963
Found on *With The Beatles*

Honed over six years of live performances, Chuck Berry's 1956 single is souped-up by the Beatles to a new and infectious level of excitement. Handclaps give a party mood and the change of tempo at 1.03 is completely missing from the original. At this point the main riff, the cymbals and the clapping stop for 15 seconds, making the re-entrance of the main guitar solo all the more arresting. George's take on the lyrics evolved through mistakes, so a 'jumping little record' becomes a 'rocking little record' and the girl wiggling like a glow-worm, becomes 'wigs', inexplicably.

   In Berry's favour his lead guitar parts are assured and flashy, whilst George's are not. Indeed, in order to get accuracy, both George's guitar intro and ending were laid down separately. His difficulty with Berry's fiddly intros can also be heard on the cack-handed 'Johnny B. Goode' from *Live at the BBC*. Months later, the Rolling Stones released their debut album, which revealed Keith Richards tackling Berry's 'Carol' with panache. The Beatles duly never recorded another Berry number with a guitar riff.

RUBBER SOUL
Recorded in 86 hours, mixed in 12 hours
Album released 3rd December 1965

Over the summer of 1965 a string of brilliant singles took pop above and beyond Tin-pan Alley clichés with profound lyrics of social reality, ennui and anguish. 'Like A Rolling Stone' by Bob Dylan, '(I Can't Get No) Satisfaction' by the Rolling Stones and 'Tracks of My Tears' by Smokey Robinson and the Miracles set new standards for anyone presumptuous enough to seek credibility with a record-buying public. With no thoughts of relinquishing their pop crowns John and Paul duly applied a greater ambition to their craft. Quick, throwaway lyrics were out and importance was placed on meaning rather than for each line to rhyme with the last; notably the first verses of 'Norwegian Wood', 'Girl' and 'In My Life' have only tenuous rhyming structures. To achieve this, on several occasions John worked through the night and to give their creations a unique arrangement, a whole day's studio time was applied to each, unlike the dashed off three-hour sessions of old. This suited John; as a deep thinker the impetus to move beyond love songs played to his strengths, while greater scrutiny in the studio brought out Paul's abilities as a musical arranger.

As part of the changing mood of the times the group now referred to death directly or obliquely ('In My Life', 'Girl', 'We Can Work It Out' and 'Run For Your Life'). John and Paul egged each other on too. The European folk ballad 'Michelle' was followed by 'Girl', the liberated woman on 'Norwegian Wood' was followed with 'Drive My Car'.

They sought new sounds to match. An overdrive of

treble on guitars on 'Nowhere Man' and on vocals for 'Girl'; deliberate sound distortion on 'I'm Looking Through You' and 'Think For Yourself' and tape-speeding on the piano solo for 'In My Life'. This willingness to distort reality owes something to marijuana and extends to the cover where their picture was stretched to make them look like giants. Yet their love of self-deprecation remained. Paul had heard a black musician refer to the Rolling Stones as 'plastic soul' and reflecting their own pretension to sound like black singers, he gave the album its punning title.

A race against time

In the space of 31 days (12th October - 11th November 1965) John and Paul wrote and recorded eight of their greatest songs*. While they would produce work of equal merit again, they would never be so intensely productive. When the group convened at Abbey Road in October, only a few songs had been written – 'Norwegian Wood', 'Run for Your Life', 'The Word' and 'Drive My Car' and there was panic over whether they could meet their November deadline whilst still retaining quality control. That they did respond shows how accustomed they had become to the heavy work schedules of live shows, interviews, filming and recording.

*Norwegian Wood, Drive My Car, Nowhere Man, In My Life, Girl, Michelle, Day Tripper and We Can Work It Out.

RUN FOR YOUR LIFE
Lennon
Recorded in five takes on 12th October 1965
Found on *Rubber Soul*

The threat of violence and superior attitude to women found on 'Run for Your Life' sit awkwardly in the Beatles' repertoire and have made it the butt of several parodies by female artists. John came to regret it, not only as it ran counter to the relationship he later had with Yoko Ono, but also as he did not take kindly to being made fun of. Months after it was released Nancy Sinatra covered it on *Boots*, an album featuring her biggest hit, 'These Boots Are Made For Walking' and a host of songs chosen to portray a tough, empowered female character at odds with the passive, delicate way women tended to be depicted in popular songs. The way 'little boy' is substituted for 'little girl' creates a delicious mischief completely missing from the Beatles' outing. John had woodenly recycled its key line about wishing to see a girl dead rather than be with another man, from Elvis Presley's early rockabilly single 'Baby, Let's Play House'. He blamed the speed of completing *Rubber Soul* for the lyrics, but his admission of a wicked and jealous mind went some way to coming to terms with the less attractive sides of his personality, a theme he would repeat on 'Getting Better' and 'Jealous Guy'.

It seems probable he wrote it with Elvis Presley in mind. Only weeks before he had had a disappointing meeting with his hero in Los Angeles. There he sought to persuade him to return to the style of his early Sun singles recorded in Memphis, but Elvis dodged the question by citing commitments to film-making. So here John recreated his own Sun Records sound, with a distinctive mix of furiously-strummed acoustic guitar and twanging electric guitar. The effect, he later admitted, was 'phoney', not least as his tenor voice carried less authority than Presley's baritone. Possibly he intended to send the track to Presley instead.

SAVOY TRUFFLE

Harrison
Basic track recorded 3rd October 1968, overdubs 5th and 11th October
Found on *The Beatles* aka The White Album

It was a rare honour to have a song about you on a Beatles' album and this tale of Eric Clapton's sweet tooth was George's way of saying thanks for a big favour. Clapton had helped bring alive 'While My Guitar Gently Weeps' after John and Paul had shown it indifference, his presence in the studio forcing them to act more 'handsomely' as George remembered.

Clapton's love of the Good News brand of chocolates is the subject matter and the glee with which George went about mocking his friend inspired a clever melody that rises in steps to a climax – a sign of the leap in skill he would soon show on 'Something'.

The powerful brass is severely compressed as if to represent the artificial flavours within the chocolates, while the not-so-subtle dig at the over-sweetness of 'Ob-la Di Ob-la Da', tells of the tensions in making *The White Album*. The 'coconut fudge', which helps blow down the 'blues', is again a nod to Clapton. Another outsider was relied on to bring it to life, stand-in producer, Chris Thomas, playing all the keyboard parts.

SEXY SADIE

Words: Lennon/Harrison   Music: Lennon/McCartney
"We had a false impression of the Maharishi, like people do of us."
John '68
Recordings on 19th July 1968 were scrapped and a new basic performance recorded in eight takes on 13th August with overdubs on 21st August
Found on *The Beatles* aka The White Album

'Trusting you made a fool of me' could have been the title for John's renunciation of the Maharishi. After eight weeks at the guru's meditation camp in India, the dawning realisation that he did not possess mystical powers made John react with all the frustration of someone who has failed to get food out of a vending machine. Full of swear words, the first draft was put together as he packed his bags to leave Rishikesh for the airport. The other Beatles, who did not share his anger, argued for a different title, George's 'Sexy Sadie' being picked. John later said he had chickened out, but a character-assassination of the Maharishi on a record sold all over the world would have been a disproportionate revenge. The ambiguous Sadie allows the listener to conjure up their own interpretation. Indeed, his band-mates were captivated by its possibilities, turning it into one of the rare *White Album* tracks where all were united in purpose. The harmony vocals are at their best and Paul's arch school hall-echoed piano is in perfect accord with John's head-teacher reprimand of the Maharishi/ Sadie for breaking the rules. A true labour of love, the group recorded 70 takes to get it right.

SGT. PEPPER'S LONELY HEARTS CLUB BAND
(album)
Recorded in 245 hours. Mixed in 59 hours.
"We were after perfection; it wasn't a question of being 99 per cent happy with something; we had to be 100 per cent happy with it."
Geoff Emerick, chief engineer.
The biggest-selling Beatles' album, worldwide sales are estimated at 32m.
First released 1st June 1967

The making of *Sgt.Pepper's* was the peak of John and Paul's love affair with the studio and the sounds they could dream up there. At last afforded an open-ended schedule, with no touring or TV commitments, hours could be spent distorting or enhancing instruments and vocals. Speakers were set at unusual angles and distances, microphones placed extra close to instruments and engineers were given outlandish requests, such as making a guitar sound like a piano.

The challenge was not shared equally. George and Ringo stood idle for longer as their band-mates perfected their masterwork and both later complained of feeling like session musicians. No doubt to their chagrin, producer, George Martin, and chief engineer, Geoff Emerick, were now being consulted more regularly than they were. John and Paul were oblivious. The delicate, telepathic way their voices intertwine on 'Getting Better' and 'She's Leaving Home' and the crucial way they stepped into help complete each other's songs shows the bubble of love they were co-habiting, each successive triumph increasing their confidence.

The energy spent overcoming the technical restraints of four-track recording equipment had its limits, however. The eight days devoted to 'Strawberry Fields Forever' and 'Penny Lane' at the start had by March and April dropped to two days for 'With A Little Help from My Friends' and 'Within You Without You' and only a day on 'Sgt Pepper's Lonely Hearts Club Band (reprise)'. The waning enthusiasm for perfection was echoed in the way Paul's grand concepts for the album went undeveloped.

The first was a pseudonym for the group under which they could play with new identities. Paul also wanted to counter the decision to end touring with the creation of a fantastical live show on disc, using spoken introductions and crowd noises. Whilst maligned now, these half-fulfilled concepts served their purpose of creating a sense that anything was possible.

SGT. PEPPER'S LONELY HEARTS CLUB BAND

McCartney
"If there was a band what would be a mad name for it?" Paul '98
A basic track was recorded on 1st February 1967 with vocal overdubs on 2nd February and brass on 6th March
Found on *Sgt. Pepper's Lonely Hearts Club Band*

French horns are traditionally used in classical music to signify a beginning or to herald the presence of a king or god. Their use here shows how excited Paul was at the quality of the album the Beatles were making – 'A Day in the Life', 'Strawberry Fields Forever' and 'Penny Lane' had all been completed in previous weeks. If the horns herald the dawn of a new standard in recorded sound the heavily-distorted guitars herald a new rock legend, Jimi Hendrix. His performances in London clubs over the winter of 1966/67 amazed audiences for the way he played rhythm and lead guitar virtually at the same time – a trick best heard on 'Foxy Lady'. Here Hendrix's thundering rhythm and quick fills, were replicated by Paul on rhythm and George on lead. Paul also goes so far as to imitate Hendrix's throaty vocals. The compliment was not lost. Hendrix included the track in his live show days after *Sgt. Pepper's* release, playing both guitar parts.

It was Paul's role, typically, to speak to live audiences and his words here recreate the illusion of a live show to make up for the Beatles' decision to end touring.

SGT. PEPPER'S LONELY HEARTS CLUB BAND (reprise)

McCartney
The second shortest Beatles' song at 1.18
Recorded in nine takes on 1st April 1967
Found on *Sgt. Pepper's Lonely Hearts Club Band*

For one evening at the close of the *Sgt. Pepper's* sessions the Beatles put aside the artistic pretensions of layer recording and simply played live. Forced to act quickly due to Paul's imminent holiday, they played a tantalisingly short piece of high-octane rock. The thrill of this exercise can be heard in their playing – particularly the vocals – making it arguably more enticing than the song it was reprising. Moving on from the Hendrix influence, the chart hit 'I'm A Man', by the Spencer Davis Group was now the template. So here likewise, stabbing bursts of music are punctuated with longer bursts of dancing percussion – cymbals, maracas and tambourine.

The group's assistant, Neil Aspinall, had suggested a

reprise as if performing a farewell to a live show. This helped patch up the album's thin concept of giving an ersatz performance to the fans who would no longer see them tour. On the last bar the band moves up several notes to end on G, neatly segueing into 'A Day in the Life', the next track, which starts on the same chord.

SHE CAME IN THROUGH THE BATHROOM WINDOW (See page 177)

SHE'S A WOMAN
Music: McCartney/Lennon   Words: McCartney/Lennon
B-side to 'I Feel Fine'
"We were so excited to say 'turn me on'," John '80.
The first Beatles' song over three minutes long and the first to use a drug reference
Written the day it was recorded 6th October 1964
Found on *Past Masters*

The Kinks' heavy metal prototype 'You Really Got Me' was in the charts when 'She's a Woman' was recorded and was the strongest of a string of Neanderthal rock sounds such as the Nashville Teens 'Tobacco Road' and The Pretty Things' 'Rosalyn' and 'Don't Bring Me Down' from the summer and autumn of 1964. This dumbed down three-chord number spoofs these with its goofy, flippant lyrics, largely composed on the spot in the studio. Paul's amusement, and no doubt admiration, is revealed in an out-take where he broke into screaming and comic vocals.

SHE LOVES YOU
McCartney/Lennon
Single released 23rd August 1963
The word 'yeah' is chanted 29 times.

Recorded on 1st July 1963
Found on *Past Masters*

From a tension-building, stumbled intro to a stark closing jazz chord, 'She Loves You' stands out as a flash of raw brilliance in the charts of 1963. Any golden oldies radio show would reveal how far it stood from the ballads and rock 'n' roll then in vogue. A mix of pace, spontaneity and a football chant of a chorus, its mood came in part from the rush in which it was made. It was then common for record companies to order new releases from their top artists as soon as their previous single started to fall down the charts. So the week after 'From Me to You' ended its two-month spell in the UK Top 10, 'She Loves You' was started in a van on the way to a gig in Newcastle-on-Tyne and then completed in a hotel bedroom.

Reflecting the rising hysteria greeting the group the lyrics are brazenly offbeat. To have apparently straight young men sing sensitive advice to another male friend defied convention. The jealousy of Elvis Presley's 'The Girl of My Best Friend' and the record which inspired Paul, Bobby Rydell's 'Forget Him' was the norm. While they are trying to lure a girl away from her boyfriend, John and Paul act as relationship counsellors. The sweet message of bringing people together touched some hidden well of emotion in the British public who made it not only the biggest selling single of its time, but gave it two separate stays at No. 1.

Its success defied one critic's initial assessment as it being their 'worst single so far'. So here 'glad' baldly rhymes with 'bad', the word 'yeah' is sung in unison 29 times and 'say' is sung as 'sayee-yay'. It is also risible that such mundane drama could be matched with glee, but John and Paul's falsetto 'wooo' before the chorus, to the climax of its inane chant makes it hard to resist.

Its tangible sense of excitement was caused in part by a

siege of fans around Abbey Road studios during its three-hour recording. At one point a teenage girl slipped through reception and burst in on the group.

In comparison with the pure live performances of their earlier singles, trickery was now coming to their aid. At 1.23, a slightly off-beat edit reveals that 'She Loves You' is, in fact, two separate takes joined together.

SHE'S LEAVING HOME

Music: McCartney   Lyrics: McCartney/Lennon
All instruments are played by session musicians
The article which inspired Paul appeared in the *Daily Mirror* on 27th February 1967, the music (strings and harp) was recorded on 17th March and the vocals on 20th March.
Found on *Sgt. Pepper's Lonely Hearts Club Band*

Paul had this written and recorded 18 days after reading of teenager, Melanie Coe's disappearance from home in a newspaper. Acting as an advocate for Coe – unlike the article in the *Daily Mirror* which empathised with her parents' fears – he uncannily worked out the full reasons for her leaving. His assumptions drew on a temporary shift of values in the Sixties where many placed spiritual and emotional needs over the material focus of their parents. Notably, Coe's father was quoted saying: "I cannot imagine why she would run away from home. She has everything here. She is very keen on clothes, but she left them all, even her fur coat." Paul imagined that she had run off with a second-hand car salesman – a 'sleazy guy with a flash car', the man in question was actually a croupier from a gambling club. Some 25 years later, the author, Steve Turner, traced Melanie Coe and amazingly she credited Paul as accurately interpreting her reasons for leaving. Though she did not leave for long: her parents discovered her two weeks later and bundled her back home.

The song is not unsympathetic to the parents: while

Paul narrates Coe's departure and tells of her desire to be free, John adds a devastating emotional edge by voicing the parents' thoughts. His lines about parental sacrifice and money were words he recalled his Aunt Mimi saying.

A delicate score beautifully evokes these emotions in a rare example of the Beatles portraying genuine heartbreak. The opening notes of the harp evoke the delicate rays of sun at day-break, the staccato violin the sudden pain of the parents. The ghostly echo applied to John's voice shows their loss too, while the slowing down of the final bar hints at sleep or at least a resignation to their grief.

SHE SAID SHE SAID

Words: Lennon/Harrison Music: Lennon
Paul does not play on this track
First started during the sessions for *Rubber Soul*
Recording started and completed 21st June 1966
Found on *Revolver*

An irritable exchange of views with the actor, Peter Fonda at a party in Los Angeles inspired John's lyrics but also the idea of discord between two guitars. On the opening riff the guitars start and end on the same note but differ in the middle. The argument occurred after they had both taken tabs of lysergic acid. John was taking the drug for only the second time and was nervous of experiencing a bad trip, when he heard Fonda gauchely boast he knew what it was like to be dead. After an accident with a gun as a youth, Fonda had temporarily passed out on the surgery table. Spooked, John quipped angrily that this was making him feel like he had not been born and said "who put all that crap in your head?"

Its first draft – a home demo of which can be found on the Internet – was simply an account of this exchange and read as 'he said'. Unsure on how it should progress, it took John months before he joined it with an idea about how everything was fine in his childhood – a recurring theme in his work. George claimed to have helped out and this partnership may have led to a subtle and temporary power shift in the group, aided in part by their shared fondness for LSD – Paul had not yet experimented. During a nine-hour recording session, Paul stormed off after a disagreement and claimed not to be on the finished track at all, with George assuming bass duties instead, Paul's voice, too, is clearly absent from the backing vocals.

SLOW DOWN

Larry Williams
Recorded in six takes on 1ˢᵗ June 1964
Found on *Past Masters*

'Mach shau' (make a show of it) was advice that had a big impact on the early Beatles' sound. Eager to retain employment as a club band in Hamburg, they learnt to add power and drama to their performances to appease the tastes of their promoter, Bruno Koschmider. The horror film-like scream John emits in the middle of 'Slow Down' at 1.40 is a great example and by comparison the scream from Larry Williams on the original is an afterthought. This focus on big emotions came at the expense of accuracy. Recorded quickly in a busy schedule, two errors at 1.15 and 2.23 occur where John muddles up the words when double-tracking his vocal. The Larry Williams original from 1958 is slicker, with tenor saxophones weaving their way round a guitar riff. Here, it is played harder, so where Williams sings it as a playful tale of a girlfriend's promiscuity, John gives it a life-or-death intensity.

SOMETHING

Harrison

"I used to be self-conscious, but now I've got fewer hang-ups about everything." George 1969

The first line was taken from the James Taylor song 'Something In The Way She Moves'.

The second most-covered Beatles' song

Thirteen takes were recorded on 16th April 1969 but scrapped. A further 36 takes on 2nd May produced the basic track (take 36) with overdubs added on 5th May, 11th July, 15th August 1969

Found on *Abbey Road*

'Something' is in keeping with the tongue-tied titles George would give to his early songs before he had settled on a chorus or key phrase as the real title. In contrast to those awkward attempts at baring his soul, this triumphs in an acceptance of an inability to succinctly express love in words. Unwittingly, this touched a nerve all around the world and has led to a long line of famous singers wanting to give their take on it too.

The relief this breakthrough brought is evident in the serene verse melody and swaggering middle eight. While the verses are essentially a personal description of his wife, the second section opens up to the listener and involves them in his revelation. For the normally private George this is an epiphany that raised him up to John and Paul's power with words. Indeed, this change of voice is similar to the contributions John made to Paul's songs, e.g. 'We Can Work It Out' and 'She's Leaving Home'. In the hands of such expressive singers as Shirley Bassey and Frank Sinatra it is open to a great range of interpretation. George's vocal, though, provides the truest version, avoiding histrionics in favour of an echo of the vulnerability evoked in the verses.

If George had learnt from John in these lyrics, then he learnt from Paul in the way the tune flows irresistibly between verse, chorus, and middle eight. Recognising this, Paul worked diligently on the track and it became the only

George Harrison song to receive more studio time than a Lennon/McCartney composition on a Beatles' album.

The Star Club tapes, Hamburg

First released April 1977 without the Beatles approval. After a court case, ownership of the tapes was passed to the Beatles in 1998.

Captured on a reel-to-reel recorder with a single microphone placed too close to George's guitar amplifier, this is not only a murky recording but a lacklustre gig*. Given at a time when the Beatles had lost interest in impressing anyone in Hamburg, listeners have reacted in kind and the tapes have become a curio that most only listen to once and then ignore.

Part of the reason for the poor sound quality is due to the style of playing; a hard machine-like approach more familiar with heavy metal or punk. Boredom with numbers they had played over and over, boredom with their audience along with a cocktail of amphetamines mixed with alcohol, the group's mechanism for coping with their long hours, appears to have led them to see how loud and fast they could play their upbeat numbers. Interspersed with easy-listening ballads such as 'Till There Was You' and 'Falling in Love Again', there is a 100mph version of 'Nothin Shakin' in one minute and 16 seconds, 'Red Hot' goes past in a blur, while 'Long Tall Sally' is eleven seconds shorter than the studio version. Whilst not as fast, there is an oddly abbreviated one minute version of 'Twist and Shout'. The unmistakeable echoes of punk are found, too, in the way Ringo's drums drive along 'I'm Going To Sit Right Down and Cry' while John's guitar is so fast on 'Roll Over Beethoven', it as if the tape has been sped up.

Another revelation is the crucial role of George. The main riffs, the solos and the melodic lines are all played by him with versatility, from rock, to Country and Western, pop and Latin. While the personalities of John and Paul dominate, the band is unthinkable without George's input, in a contrast to the following years where his role was diminished.

The tapes offer a candid view of the early working relationship between John and Paul. John is drunk, belligerent, childish, and often talking gibberish on stage, whilst Paul is the pacifier, the PR man diffusing awkward situations. After an aggressive German heckle, he responds in a heightened gentlemanly voice: "Good evening sir, how are you? You seem rather..(*unintelligible*)". He makes announcements, "The next one is a special request from Inge for a cha-cha-cha". There is even some subtle humour, he introduces 'Kansas City' as "Kansas Stadt, a Bach fugue in B minor" and 'To Know Her Is To Love Her' as 'To Know It Is To Love Her'.

Paul needed a sense of humour to cope with John who tries to put him off singing 'I Remember You' and 'Till There Was You'. John baits the audience too, calling them "schweinhunds" and singing "shitty" on 'Shimmy Like Kate'. He talks nonsense too, safe in the knowledge the audience cannot fully understand. He says: "You lost the war but you are taking it at a good time". Indeed, there is a joke alluding to the language barrier; "I don't know whether you understand me or not", he says repeatedly.

*The recording was originally billed as being from New Year's Eve 1962, but it is now believed to come from several performances at the end of December.

STRAWBERRY FIELDS FOREVER

Lennon
Single first released 13th February 1967
Recordings made on 24th and 28th November 1966 were scrapped. A

basic track was completed to satisfaction on 29th November. A new backing track was recorded on 8th December to which overdubs were added on 9th, 15th and 21st December. On 22nd December 1966 a join was made of the first minute of the November track with everything recorded in December forming the second half.
Found on *Magical Mystery Tour*

Just weeks after the ignominious end to the Beatles' last world tour John sat in a chair on a film set and had his long locks of hair cut into a short back and sides. Curiously, the new face in the mirror was one he had not seen for 10 years. The cropped look was created to fit his screen role as a soldier in the film 'How I Won the War' but for him it would have conjured up the clean-cut schoolboy he was before fame, rock 'n' roll and responsibility. Seeing his face like this each day he found himself reminiscing, during the long hours on the set, about his childhood hideaway in the gardens of a large neo-gothic house close to his home in Liverpool, called Strawberry Field. The grand styling of the property must have appeared as the likely backdrop for one of the Lewis Carroll 'Alice' stories he loved as a boy – literally a place where nothing had to be real and life was easier, as he states, with closed eyes and where there is nothing to be hung for.*

These happy memories were an escape from a more pressing reality – John was contemplating a role for himself beyond the Beatles. The tension of a harrowing world tour had left a chill with his band-mates. They had endured death threats in Tokyo and a scramble to escape a government mob in Manila, but then had to face more death threats and empty seats in the USA – a country which once welcomed them wholeheartedly – due to John's reckless statement about the Beatles being more popular than Jesus Christ. In public, Paul, George and Ringo argued how the logic of what he had said was not anti-Christian, but in private they let him know of their resentment. Years later, it was left to Yoko Ono to tell of how hurt John had been by this.

For a while, hiding behind a persona on screen appeared an attractive alternative career, but he soon became tired by the lack of control and, bored with the endless waiting, he fell into a catatonic state of contemplation on the set of 'How I Won the War', once it reached southern Spain in October 1966. His chauffeur recalled the normally laconic John as barely uttering a word to him whilst in Spain and the verses he wrote there over six weeks for 'Strawberry Fields Forever', read like a conversation he was having with himself rather than the listener, even to the extent of adding an 'err' between words. Indeed, he later referred to it as psychoanalysis set to music. The verses map out his crisis, whilst the chorus, with its invitation for us all to join him in his longing for a trouble-free make-believe world, reads like the answer.

Its creation brought him some measure of acceptance of his role as a Beatle, but, symbolically, he gave up his mop-top hairstyle and grew a moustache. No more would he wear contact lenses to maintain his public image either, instead he wore the spectacles that had helped stylise his film role as a doomed soldier. Pointedly, the song title offers an alternate world view to the banners held by his fans, which proclaimed 'The Beatles Forever'.

Days after returning to London he was in the studio bringing his vision to life. The first run-through featured the other-worldly sound of a mellotron, a newly-invented proto-synthesiser that could be used only in 11-second bursts, as well as long spooky notes on slide guitar. As this was their first album made without the urgency of a deadline, they were afforded the luxury of a second attempt at getting it right. Imperiously, John ordered strings and brass for a bolder, more cacophonic rendition, but then on deeming this only partly right he asked George Martin to join the two very different versions together. The halves were a note apart, but by speeding up the first and slowing down the second, their keys met. John's speeded-up voice takes on a boyish quality in the first half, whilst in the second, one minute in, his slowed-down voice hints at sleep and a fantastical dream ride. What could have been a fool's errand for the sound engineers opened up a new dimension in recorded sound. That so many have sought to emulate 'Strawberry Fields Forever' but so few have succeeded shows how fortuitous the discovery was. It was also decisive in demonstrating that lengthy experimentation produced results, setting the benchmark for Sgt.Pepper's.

*This has an uncanny, but surely subconscious, parallel with the message in the lyrics to 'Over the Rainbow' – which had once been part of the Beatles' repertoire.

The intro and the outro

The coda to 'Strawberry Fields Forever' bears a close resemblance to 'Caroline No' by the Beach Boys. Both are tangential to the song and both fade in and out. On 'Caroline No' there is a ringing bell and a train running over tracks, whilst on 'Strawberry Fields' a single note is played on guitar not unlike a bell ringing and the drums imitate the clatter of train wheels over points. The only difference is a dog barking on 'Caroline No' and John intoning the nonsense 'cranberry sauce'.

The link between 'Yesterday' and 'Strawberry Fields Forever'

One is a beautiful melody with a clear message, the other a psychedelic maelstrom. The idea that they share a theme is not obvious, but on investigation, compelling. Paul's lament at saying something wrong is popularly believed to refer to his first words after finding out his mother had died, "What are we going to do without her money?" Her sudden death broke the idyll of his home life at age 14. 'Strawberry Fields Forever' followed John's regret over the storm caused by his observation in an interview that "the Beatles were bigger than Christ". As a contrast to the scandal his comments caused in the USA, he harked back to the innocence of his childhood and the make-believe world he created at the Salvation Army home at Strawberry Field in Liverpool. The gardens, which he would climb a wall to reach, literally represented a 'hideaway', a word used on 'Yesterday'. Paul's lyrics do not explicitly state childhood, but the reference to games and play hints at it.

The happiness both songs reminisce about is used as a contrast to the crises and guilt that befell them. Paul sings of being half the person he used to be, while John tells of finding it difficult to be 'someone'. Both make odd assertions of faith in the past. Paul says yesterday is something he believes in, while John says Strawberry Fields is forever.

Both are among their most complex chord structures, as if they needed the fullest palette of notes to do justice to their emotions. Both were intensely personal, with neither calling on their partner for help in writing. Both lyrics were written while relaxing abroad, John in southern Spain and Paul in Portugal, almost as if they needed to step out of their current lives to put their past in context.

SUN KING/ MEAN MR MUSTARD/ POLYTHENE PAM

Lennon

SHE CAME IN THROUGH THE BATHROOM WINDOW

McCartney
'Sun King'/ 'Mean Mr Mustard' basic track recorded 24th July 1969 with overdubs on 25th July, 30th July.
'Polythene Pam'/ 'She Came In Through the Bathroom Window' basic track recorded 25th July 1969 with overdubs on 28th July, 30th July.
Found on *Abbey Road*

Creative people will often doodle before they can settle down to more serious work. The act warms up the mind and frees it of extraneous ideas. As such these song doodles are full of whimsical nonsense and parody. 'Sun King' mocks John's lack of understanding of foreign languages. 'Mean Mr Mustard', in its deadpan tone, mocks the mundanity of a man depicted in a newspaper who had become obsessed with saving money. These were engineered as a single performance and likewise, Mr Mustard's sister is name-checked as Pam to help link it to the next unified doodles, 'Polythene Pam' and 'She Came In Through the Bathroom Window'. 'Pam' alludes to a fan from the Cavern, nicknamed Polythene Pat, and is combined with a memory of a night of lust in the early days of Beatlemania. Its use of the phrase 'killer diller' comes from Bo Diddley's 'The Story of Bo Diddley' where it was used as a term of sexual prowess. As John says, his creation ought to have appeared in the *News of The World*, a British Sunday paper that thrived on scandal stories. The last doodle tells of a group of fans who used a ladder to climb into Paul's London house. One got in through his bathroom window and went downstairs to let the others in. Paul played detective by quizzing the fans who congregated outside his house to get stolen photos and clothes returned. All four of these scraps are inconsequential on their own, but became greater than the sum of their parts through the attention given to blending them together, and the evident satisfaction the group had in achieving this.

A TASTE OF HONEY
Written by Bobby Scott and Ric Marlow
Recorded in seven takes on 11th February 1963
Found on *Please Please Me*

A lovely ballad beautifully sung, or a piece of schmaltz out of place in the Beatles' repertoire? Such were the differences of opinion that Paul had to drag a member of The Merseybeats into the dressing room at the Cavern to help persuade John of the song's merit after they had played it live for the first time.* John accepted defeat with poor grace, as he would subsequently take delight in sabotaging it. At the Star Club in December 1962 a recording captures Paul giving the audience a hint of what will follow by stating, "something that John will hate...'A Taste of Honey'." John, responds unconvincingly "No... I love it." But as anticipated, midway through, he shouts "Shut up talking" – as the hubbub of the club can be heard over this quiet ballad, which causes Paul to snigger, giving John victory. More sabotage can be detected six weeks later in the studio. Some over-earnest backing vocals (especially at 1.20) suggest John is gesticulating to make Paul fluff his lines again in the studio.

'A Taste of Honey' was a cover of Lenny Welch's silky violin-led original, which Paul first saw Pete MacLaine, a fellow Liverpool singer, perform live.

* Spencer Leigh, *Lets Go Down The Cavern* 1982.

TAXMAN
Words: Harrison/Lennon   Music: Harrison/McCartney
Basic track recorded 21st April 1966, overdubs 22nd April, 16th May
Found on *Revolver*

Pop took an odd turn when Mick Jagger told of how his heart was black, The Who declared a desire for an early death and Bob Dylan said that all of us should get 'stoned'*. These utterances in the first few months of 1966 were soon joined by one sung in character as a taxman who relishes taking money from the rich. George's complaint was made 20 days after a British general election which saw the Labour Party, with its policy of making the highest earners pay a 95%

income tax, re-elected. He had sat down at the beginning of the year to work out his true wealth and to his horror, as the lyrics state, he was paying 19 pounds in tax for every 20 he earned after allowances. John was intrigued enough to contribute the line about declaring the pennies that traditionally were placed on the eyes of the dead to pay their way into heaven and he possibly added more. He later bitterly contrasted the help he gave here with the lack of recognition given to him in George's autobiography *I Me Mine*. That Paul leads the caustic arrangement suggests he felt the pain of these taxes too. Underneath George's mannered count-in, you can hear him give the real count-in for the band. His leaping bass dominates, benefiting from the high volume offered by the advent of new compressors at Abbey Road studios, as does his distorted guitar solo, which, though unremarkable today, was at the time astonishing; this is in effect rich man's punk rock. For those not in this salary range there was little sympathy. 'Sunny Afternoon', a summer No.1 for The Kinks, was also sung in character, but as a mocking lament of a lord who is being forced to cut back.

*'Paint It Black' by the Rolling Stones, 'My Generation' by The Who and 'Rainy Day Women # 12 and 35' by Bob Dylan.

TELL ME WHAT YOU SEE (See page 56)

TELL ME WHY
Lennon
Paul speculated that John was writing about a row he'd had with his wife.
Recorded in eight takes on 27th February 1964
Found on *A Hard Day's Night*

John recalled this as something he 'knocked off' to appease the producers of the *A Hard Day's Night* film, who requested another upbeat song. It is probable it was written a night or two before recording as, of all the six songs written to meet United Artists requirements, its lyrics are the least logical. John demands to know why a loved one has 'lied' and 'cried', but then recounts how he will 'cry' if his loved one leaves him. All this talk of tears is paired with the joyful mood requested by United Artists. Picking up on this absurd mismatch John and Paul's comical choirboy falsettos mock their own creation.

THANK YOU GIRL

Lennon/McCartney
B-side to 'From Me To You'
Basic track recorded 5th March 1963, harmonica overdubbed 13th March
Found on *Past Masters*

John and Paul took two attempts at perfecting a shameless promise of eternal love to their new fans, with 'From Me to You' and 'Thank You Girl'. They then sought opinion as to which was best from the artists they were then on tour with. Backing their own hunch, 'Thank You Girl' was less popular and by the sound of it given little studio time. Their manic and poorly synchronised vocals suggest neither could concentrate on the task at hand, thrilled no doubt that minutes before they had recorded their next hit single, 'From Me to You'.

THERE'S A PLACE

Lennon/McCartney
John and Paul disagreed on who wrote most of this. Paul said he did, but John claimed credit for the lyrics.
Recorded in seven takes on 11th February 1963
Found on *Please Please Me*

Under-rehearsed and not yet warmed up, the first song recorded for *Please Please Me* is messy but enthralling. The vocals strain to hit the right notes and retain the tempo, whilst at 0.53 Ringo stumbles over a beat. Yet the eerie way John and Paul's voices combine on the words 'mine' and 'time' and the effect of occasionally adding George's harmony vocal are magical. They were so annoyed at underselling it, the group worked through their lunch hour rehearsing their subsequent numbers.

It was one of their boldest lyrics, John making the startling admission for its day, that when he was alone in his thoughts there was no such thing as time. This expanded on a theme from 'There's A Place for Us' from the musical *West Side Story*. Stephen Sondheim's lyrics refer not only to a special place for two lovers, but also a 'time' for them too. However, one suspects John was not thinking about romance so much as an exploration of his imagination – an early hint of psychedelia.

THINGS WE SAID TODAY

McCartney
Written below deck on a boat in the Caribbean
Recorded in three takes on 2nd June 1964
Found on *A Hard Day's Night*

Paul was fascinated by the way 'Besame Mucho' switched from the minor chord of a key on the verses to its major for the chorus. Its minor chords convey caution ('if you should leave me'), while the major chords convey positivity – 'besame mucho' tr. 'kiss me a lot', and 'love me forever'. Similarly here on A minor, Paul speculates of what will happen to him and his girlfriend Jane Asher if they are apart, before, on a reassuring A major, he describes himself as 'lucky' and tells how their love will always 'stay'. However, while 'Besame Mucho' sticks to standard themes, Paul is more ambitious. Instead of a fear of parting, he imagines looking back at a special moment from the future, treasuring it for what it is worth.

Equally, the chords are more advanced, the curious C, C7, F, B flat refrain ('someday…') is added to the end of each verse and a string of sevenths to the main break out section, giving a bluesy touch missing from 'Besame Mucho'.

THINK FOR YOURSELF

Harrison
Recorded on 8th November 1965
Found on *Rubber Soul*

Echoing Bob Dylan's 'It Ain't Me Babe', George tells of how he has changed but his partner has not and how they must move on. Dylan's relationship song has been interpreted as a veiled swipe at musical purists who knocked him for abandoning folk music and George explained 'Think for Yourself' as a veiled swipe at the government. It actually makes more sense as a pep talk he was having with himself. Still in the shadow of Lennon/McCartney, the answer he says is to follow one's own path and destiny. The use of a fuzz box on bass makes this desire to be different clear, if without subtlety.

THIS BOY

Lennon/ McCartney
B-side to 'I Want To Hold Your Hand'
William Mann, the music critic for the Times famously praised 'This Boy' for its *'chains of pan-diatonic clusters'* – John said he had no idea what Mann was on about, saying that pan-diatonic sounded like an exotic bird. A text book description of pan-diatonic is music that uses the notes of the diatonic scale in dissonant combinations without conventional resolutions and/or without standard chord progressions, sometimes to the extent that no single pitch is felt as a tonic.
Recorded in 17 takes on 17th October 1963
Found on *Past Masters*

A highlight of the Beatles' early live shows were the three-voice harmonies on slow numbers such as 'To Know Him Is to Love Him'. Keen to replicate these they created their own purpose-built ballad here. Its strength is in the flipping of octaves between lead and backing vocals. John takes the low notes for the verses while Paul and George are an octave above. On the middle eight, Paul and George switch to a low bass hum, while John makes his emotional plea not to be spurned by hitting the highest and loudest notes of his range. All else was an afterthought. The tune was simply borrowed from 'You Don't Understand Me', the B-side to Bobby Freeman's hit, 'Do You Wanna Dance'. It features the same bass line, the same lilting four-chord trick (D – Bm – G – A) loved by doo-wop and acapella groups and a searing, soulful vocal. The only difference is the positivity of the Lennon/McCartney lyrics. John credited Smokey Robinson as an influence too, and he may have been thinking of the hopeful message of '(You Can) Depend on Me' too.

TICKET TO RIDE

Lennon/McCartney
The first Beatles' A side to breach three minutes at 3.01.
First released on 9th April 1965.
Recorded on 15th February 1965
Found on *Help!*

To have Paul acting as his musical arranger must have been a constant thrill for John; here his monotone verses and simplistic riff are transformed by a beat which to this day can flummox many a drummer. The repetition of the riff never gets worn out, as each note is counter-pointed by the loping five-part drum pattern. The box of tricks extended to a surprise ending with a raised tempo, a discordant note on bass to offset the opening A chord, gloriously-poised drum rolls and a vigorously shaken tambourine. A less obvious detail is the distorted rhythm guitar which is pushed back in the mix – John recalled he would have liked this louder and referred to 'Ticket To Ride' as one of the "earliest heavy metal songs ever made". Subjugated to the arrangement, the words main role is rhythmic. The emphasis in the first line is all on the hard sounds, 'tthinkkahm', 'ggonnabbe', 'sadduh', 'tterday'. This serves as a layer of percussion to the click-clack of the instruments that chug along like the train taking his girl away from him. Cover versions have largely ignored this. Notably the Carpenters' sought to evoke the sadness of the words, but as 'ticket to ride' was a pun, it suggests they held little meaning – Ryde was a town in the Isle of Wight in England which John and Paul had once visited on holiday.

TILL THERE WAS YOU

Meredith Wilson
"This next tune is a special request for Inga for a cha-cha-cha (sic)."
Paul's introduces 'Till There Was You' at the Star Club, Hamburg, December 1962.
Recordings on 18th July 1963 were rejected. A remake took place on 30th July
Found on *With The Beatles*

Before record royalties paid their wages some of the best money the Beatles could earn was playing in the up-market dance venues around Liverpool. To win these bookings there had to be a planned set list, suits and ties, plus lounge music such as 'Till There Was You'. The polite musicianship and clear diction of their version impressed George Martin when he first heard their tapes and it was duly deemed suitable for the Queen Mother and Princess Margaret at the Royal Variety Show in November 1963. Paul still plays it to this day, but the references to 'wonderful roses' and 'fragrant meadows' were not to John's taste. At the Star Club on New Year's Eve 1962, he turned it into a joke by reciting the lines in a deadpan way after Paul had sung them.

The track was found on Peggy Lee's album *Latin À La Lee,* whose sleeve notes describe it as 'Broadway hits with an Afro-Cuban beat'. Lee's version is a spoof. The staid original from the musical *The Music Man* is sung by a librarian to a professor, but Lee gives it a louche, breathy vocal and the sultry rhythm of the Cuban dance, the cha-cha-cha. For Paul, it was Lee's arrangement that caught his imagination and he sings it straight missing the joke entirely. Though to the group's credit, the piano and flute from Lee's version is cleverly transposed onto Spanish guitar which must have taken weeks of practice.

TOMORROW NEVER KNOWS

Words: Lennon   Music: Lennon/McCartney
'The void is not nothingness. The void is beginning and end itself. Unobstructed; shining, thrilling, blissful.' Timothy Leary, *The Psychedelic Experience*.
John changed the title from 'The Void' to 'Tomorrow Never Knows', feeling it had got overly serious.
Recorded 6th-7th April 1966 with overdubs on 22nd April
Found on *Revolver*

After several years of mass adulation it suddenly became exciting for John to see the reaction on people's faces when they heard a song the exact opposite of what was expected. As such, the incredible jump from early hits such as 'She Loves You' to 'Tomorrow Never Knows' was part of his design. In doing so the song broke a string of song-writing conventions that were previously sacrosanct. The Beatles had often privately joked to themselves about the absurdity of making a song with one chord and here they did just that. For good measure the lines do not rhyme and the weird sounds they enjoyed creating on their open reel tape recorders, which they had previously only ever played at home were added too.

Such confounding of expectations coincided with

John's love affair with the drug LSD. Enthralled by the alternative perspectives it gave on life he sought to spread its message. Inspiration came from the maverick US psychologist, Timothy Leary, who had the same idea in 1964 when he published a pamphlet entitled *The Psychedelic Experience.* John borrowed key phrases from Leary's manifesto, in particular the intonation that the loss of ego through LSD is not about dying, but being reborn. The instruction to relax and explore our thoughts is more typical of John, whilst elsewhere there are textbook accounts of LSD, where the user becomes so sensitive to colours that they appear to speak. Leary's work itself was framed on *the Tibetan Book of the Dead,* a guide for monks on how to help those on the verge of death into a peaceful afterlife.

This eastern philosophy begged for the use of sitar and tambura for authenticity while the drum beat is tribal, like that for a Native American war dance or a shamanistic ritual. For good measure John envisaged Tibetan monks chanting, with himself sounding, as he remembered, like the Dalai Lama on a hilltop. The request was outside of George Martin's experience and John lacked the musical palette to suggest an alternative. Rising to the challenge, Paul championed the use of sound effects he had already created at home. Played backwards, speeded up and slowed down, these tapes are a mix of the bizarre and the nightmarish. This appealed to John's desire to shock, but he later regretted not using the monks' chants. His intention surely had been an inviting, intoxicating message, but Paul's sounds, often likened to monstrous seagulls, seem to tell the listener to turn back and resist John's beckoning.

Is the messianic figure in The Who's rock opera *Tommy* based on John Lennon?

Pete Townsend created rock's most intriguing concept album in late 1968 with the tale of a boy from a troubled home who becomes a superstar. Uncannily this character has many similarities to John Lennon. Tommy suffers psychologically from the loss of his father when aged 5 and goes blind ('Eyesight To The Blind'). John, too, lost contact with his father at the age of 5 and would often forgo the glasses he needed for acute short-sightedness. Both had parents or parental figures who despair for their future until a life-changing experience (rock 'n' roll for John, pinball for Tommy), leads to both becoming undisputed champions. Both were in thrall to LSD ('Acid Queen') and sought help from all manner of doctors and gurus ('Miracle Cure'/ the Maharishi and transcendental meditation) after which they encourage others to share this experience ('Welcome'/'Tommy's Holiday Camp'). The latter could be either the Beatles' trip to Rishikesh, India, which Ringo memorably compared to Butlins, or the launch of Apple with its invitation to other artists to come and join them. Tommy's call to his followers to recreate his deaf, dumb and blind state is remarkably similar to 'Tomorrow Never Knows' call to turn off thoughts and surrender to the void. The media cynicism to the Beatles' embracing of Eastern mysticism, coupled with John's own rejection of the Maharishi ('We're Not Going To Take It') is the conclusion. All these events took place prior to the start date for the recording of Tommy in September 1968 and it seems likely Townsend took inspiration from the biography of the Beatles, published that summer by Hunter Davies, which revealed much about John's early life.

TWIST AND SHOUT

Written by Bert Berns

"There was one song that always caused a furore in the Cavern – 'Twist and Shout,'" George Martin '79

On the vocal crescendo, John sings the first 'aah', George the second and Paul the third, fourth and fifth.

Recorded in one take on 11th February 1963.

Found on *Please Please Me*

Accounts of those who saw the Beatles live in small venues 1961-62 tell more than of a band that could play well, but of an out-of-body experience; "I was in a trance for days", "the place went bananas", "they were raw and animal" *. The studio performance of 'Twist and Shout' captures this headiness, not as a call to try the latest dance craze, but, as many parents feared, an incitement for teenagers to reach a state of hysteria. This is matched in the playing, Ringo thumps the snare drum with an aggression not characteristic of him and George plucks the opening riff with force. Indeed, all were playing with drive, power and fluidity after 10 hours recording their debut album, all except for John's vocals which were worn out and suffering from a cold. Struggling and already dripping with sweat from his exertions, Paul and George's backing vocals are sung with enormous passion to cover for his distress. The vocals audibly deteriorate over the course of the recording. The first verse is gravelly, but by 0.25 he is struggling to form the words, and at 1.01 his voice is close to falling apart, but the 15 second instrumental break allows him back with a little more strength. One take was all he could cope with, but it was clear the performance was only seconds away from being lost.

'Twist and Shout' was a cash-in on the twist craze of 1961, by New York song-writer, Bert Berns, under the pseudonym of Medley/Russell. Its first recording by The Top Notes was so shambolic that Berns tried again with The Isley Brothers, who made it a No. 17 hit in the US in 1962. Here it became an evocation of a Latin street carnival, with trumpets playing the main riff and a tambourine backing the beat, suggesting the colour and noise of the parade. Nothing about it suggests the heavy rock of the Beatles' version which was developed in Hamburg, where audiences appreciated a cruder, louder version of US pop. According to Gerry Marsden of Gerry and the Pacemakers, the Beatles 'nicked' it after seeing fellow Merseybeat group, King Size Taylor and the Dominoes, perform it live. Taylor had a contact in the USA who would send over records before their release in the UK and before other groups could hear them. The Beatles spent some time with the Dominoes at the Star Club in Hamburg and one innovation they may have copied was the ploy of repeating the rising crescendo of voices at the song's close. By contrast the original version by The Isley Brothers simply fades out.

*Spencer Leigh 'Let's Go Down The Cavern' 1982

TWO OF US

McCartney
Recorded on 31st January 1969
Found on *Let It Be*

This piece of effervescent joy shone through the misery of the *Let It Be* sessions. In the previous months, Paul's relationship with Linda Eastman had blossomed through a shared love of driving into the countryside with the aim of getting lost and then finding their way home. A relief from the tensions of recording and business deals, on one such trip, whilst parked next to a field, Paul came to write 'Two of Us'. At the time, Canned Heat's feel-good hit 'Going up the Country' was being played on the radio and its message of getting away from the city to a location in the country is near identical. On the verses, Paul shared vocals with John on a single microphone, which has led to the belief he is referring to their partnership too, on the lines about how far their shared memories stretched back. Indeed, as a sign their partnership was still functioning, John used this tale of free-wheeling travel as a blueprint for 'The Ballad of John and Yoko' months later.

WAIT

McCartney/Lennon
Written in the Bahamas, while filming *Help!*
Basic track recorded 17th June 1965, with overdubs on 11th November.
Found on *Rubber Soul*

The use of a different chord for virtually every word marks this out as something special even if its reassuring tale of fidelity did not. Written in the spring and basically recorded in the summer, it sat on the shelf until November 1965, when the group had started exploring more complex emotions. So, for balance, the Beatles went about optimising the edginess of the chords instead, through a set of creepy-sounding overdubs. Where the vocals warmly tell of coming home, the shivering use of tremolo on the guitar strings resonate loneliness, whilst the vigorously-shaken maracas suggest tension and escape. And where the last line originally conjured up longing, the dying guitar notes imbue the final word 'alone' with dread, after which a tambourine shakes like a tail twitch of a rattlesnake.

WE CAN WORK IT OUT

Words: McCartney/ Lennon   Music: McCartney/Lennon/ Harrison
It was George's suggestion for the song's switch to waltz time
John plays harmonium
Double A-side 'Day Tripper' released on 3rd December 1965
Basic recording made 20th October 1965 with overdubs on 29th October.
Found on *Past Masters*

Is there a more compact A-side in pop music? In two minutes and 12 seconds there are four verses, four choruses, two middle eights and a coda. There is even room for two changes to waltz-time. The pace matches the urgency of its 'life's too short' message. A harmonium, which happened to be sitting in the studio, was seized upon and its slow tones are a delicious contrast to the furiously-strummed acoustic guitar and tambourine. The contrast is in the vocals too, where the mix of views is like a mini-opera. Paul's reasoned response to a row with Jane Asher makes up the verses, while John's cautionary middle eight urges against wasting time. This had a personal resonance for him as he wrote it a week after turning 25 and like many pop stars he did not expect to sustain a career past 30, greeting his birthdays with increasing concern.

Paul's optimism echoes the can-do spirit of John's 'Nowhere Man', which was recorded the day before. The similarity suggests a band so close they were sharing the same thoughts and values.

WHAT GOES ON
Words: Lennon/McCartney/Starkey   Music: Lennon/McCartney
Recorded in one take 4th November 1965
Found on *Rubber Soul*

'What Goes On' was a piece of teenage angst that John had half written in the 1950s. In the rush to complete *Rubber Soul* he dug it out and handed it to Paul to polish, who, with Ringo, added some lines. In all probability this was done with minutes to spare as the second verse with its reference to the 'tides of time' is nonsensical and the third verse contradictory. A slim arrangement too is laid bare by Ringo's inability to raise his register fully for the chorus. Aware of its shortcomings the group could only bear performing a single listless take; John's ragged rhythm and Paul's simple bass line may well have been created on the spot. The most effort comes from George, whose lead guitar fashions a Carl Perkins-like commentary on the vocal melody. As if as an apology, Paul put great effort into Ringo's next studio recording, 'Yellow Submarine', arranging it so the whole group carry the chorus.

WHAT YOU'RE DOING

Music: McCartney   Lyrics: McCartney/Lennon
The 12-string guitar riff was used by The Byrds as inspiration on 'Mr Tambourine Man'.
Twelve takes from 29th and 30th September 1964 were scrapped. Remade in six takes on 26th October 1964.
Found on *Beatles For Sale*

This is an experiment with extremes of pace, tone and octave, that uses the studio as a laboratory. A seven-second drum intro is followed by a high-pitched guitar riff. The highest vocal notes are met with low notes on bass and vice versa. When Paul imploringly sings the words, 'look', 'please' and 'you', at the start of each verse, he and John jointly shout it as an overdub*. An over-eager set of fingers was not far from the mixing board too. Sound levels for the guitar riff drop dramatically at 0.30, whilst re-emerging loudly at 1.18. Another device is the stop-start of the band which on several occasions leaves Paul's voice hanging in mid-air, as if to emphasise his struggle to keep up with the girl in the song who has got him running. John and Paul were both quick to dismiss the track when asked to recall their back catalogue as perhaps they felt the end result did not justify the time spent and the attention to detail.

*'Stay' by Maurice Williams and the Zodiacs, which the Beatles played live in Hamburg, used an imperative word sung forcefully by the backing singers at the start of each verse, too.

WHEN I GET HOME

Lennon
Recorded in 11 takes on 2nd June 1964
Found on *A Hard Day's Night*

With the Beatles days away from two long overseas tours it was fitting that they should record a song entitled 'When

I Get Home' for their British fans. 'I'll Be Back' and 'Anytime At All' recorded on the same 1st and 2nd June 1964 sessions also allude to their absence. But that this is so clearly rushed blunts its sincerity. The vocals on the intro are off key and John's heroic lead vocal cannot cover up for a set of lyrics which seem unsure whether to be serious or comical.

WHEN I'M 64

McCartney
When Paul wrote this aged 16 he envisaged it being used in a musical. A basic track was recorded on 6th December 1966 with overdubs on 8th, 20th, 21st December
Found on *Sgt. Pepper's Lonely Hearts Club Band*

Legend has it that Paul would play this on piano at the Cavern whenever the amplifiers cut out, due to the humidity of the poorly-ventilated venue 'shorting' the electricity. His line about mending fuses refers to the times he sang it in the dark and it is hard to imagine a group of men either side of 20 finding this anything but a laugh. When it was polished up for *Sgt. Pepper's* Paul worked with George Martin on a 1930's style score of clarinets, strings and ever-so-precise bass, while the lead vocal was sped up to mimic the whiny pitch of records from that era and John dreamt up the playful jazz guitar. However, John and George were uncomfortable that much of the joke had been lost and John later said dismissively: "I would never dream of writing a tune like that."

WHILE MY GUITAR GENTLY WEEPS

Harrison
George's lyric about a love that has been sleeping echoes Donovan's recent 'Hurdy Gurdy Man' which refers to truth buried in a hundred year's sleep.
Recordings on 25th July 1968, 16th August and 3rd September were all

scrapped. The basic track was made on 5th September and completed with overdubs, including Eric Clapton's guitar on 6th September 1968
Found on *The Beatles* aka The White Album

Little much was known of the disdain with which George's songs were treated by John and Paul until the publication of transcripts from the *Let It Be* rehearsals*. These show how George had to fight against the indifference of both before getting one of his compositions on tape and from what is known of 'While My Guitar Gently Weeps' he was facing the same struggle during the making of the *White Album*.

Over three recording sessions he failed to get a satisfactory take of what he knew to be a breakthrough in his songwriting. After giving up on the idea of a backwards guitar solo, he by-passed John and Paul and invited Eric Clapton, then lead guitarist of Cream, to provide the missing piece of magic. A skilful piece of manoeuvring, George said later "It made them all try a bit harder; they were all on their best behaviour." For many, Clapton's solo, with its beautiful, long, sustained notes is one of the greatest in rock 'n' roll and it has become an irresistible challenge for other guitarists.** However, the delicate acoustic demo version (from 25th July) also has its fans, not least for the intricate arpeggio that was buried in the studio version. The orchestral overdubs given by George Martin for the *Love* album emphasise the demo's delicate poetry instead.

Martin's re-working is interesting as he was on holiday when the final studio version was made and it lacks his usual production values. Notably, Paul's double tracked bass has a crude sound, while the high-pitched drone of organ and wailing vocals have been ignored by cover versions.

*As documented in *Get Back:The Beatles' Let It Be Disaster* by Doug Sulphy and Ray Schweighardt (1998)
** Notable cover versions include Santana, Peter Frampton, Jeff

Healy and the pyrotechnic display given by Prince at George Harrison's entry into the Rock 'n' Roll Hall of Fame in 2004. All typically extend their versions to give more space for the solo.

Noodle soup

Just under a third of all Beatles' songs contain a guitar solo – 67 of the 209 songs released during their life as a group. The majority are played by George, but four are by John ('Get Back', 'You Can't Do That', 'For You Blue', 'Honey Pie') three by Paul ('Drive My Car', 'Taxman' and 'Good Morning Good Morning') and one by Eric Clapton ('While My Guitar Gently Weeps').

A further four are shared – 'And Your Bird Can Sing' George and Paul play simultaneously, on 'Birthday' John and Paul take solos, on 'Yer Blues' John takes the first solo and George, by the sound of it, takes the second, while on 'The End' John, Paul and George all play short passages in a combined solo. It is not clear who plays what on 'Back in the USSR', but George is almost certainly joined here by John or Paul.

The longest solo is Clapton's at over one minute, the shortest is at six seconds on 'I'll Follow The Sun'. Perhaps the most interesting is the 12 second backwards solo on 'I'm Only Sleeping', it took George three hours to find the rhythm and the right notes to match music travelling in the opposite direction.

The typical solo can be found between one minute and one minute 20 seconds into a Beatles track, usually after a couple of verses and a chorus or two. Some of the notable exceptions are the solo at the end of 'Girl' and those used on the fade outs to 'Taxman' and 'And Your Bird Can Sing'. Arguably the most unfortunate solo is that on 'All You Need Is Love' where George playing live in the studio hits a duff note. The best is a matter of taste but the exhilarating solo on 'Hey Bulldog' has to be up there.

THE WHITE ALBUM (official title The Beatles)
"The tension album," Paul '85
"During my many visits to Abbey Road during the summer and autumn of 1968, all the old fun, laughter and camaraderie seemed

conspicuous by their absence." Pete Shotton, close friend of John Lennon, '84.
Recorded in 559 hours May-October 1968, mixed in 102 hours.
Album released November 22nd 1968.

After two years of layer-recording slick and fantastical sounds on which his limited musicianship was exposed, John fought for a return to working live. On his first day back in the studio he brazenly informed anyone who would listen that he did not want to record any more 'shit' like *Sgt. Pepper's*. To get his way he shouted and swore and sought the opinion of George Martin so little, he recalled it as an album that had not really been produced. Confidence came from now having Yoko Ono by his side, as a lover, muse and *agent provocateur*. Paul and George seethed at this breach of their closed circle and her insensitivity to their status, but it did not stop them continuing to create cutting edge music. Playing again as a unit created the vibrancy of 'Hey Jude', 'Revolution', 'Helter Skelter', 'Happiness Is a Warm Gun' and 'Sexy Sadie' and led to the exciting switches of time signatures of 'Birthday' and 'Everybody's Got Something to Hide Except For Me and My Monkey', but it was hard work getting there. In layer-recording only a good take of drums, bass and rhythm guitar were needed, before adding the overdubs one at a time. Now, sometimes 100 takes were made to ensure vocals or intricate solos were satisfactory. Even then – at times consciously – jokes, asides, stray notes and beats, count-ins and chatter all make it into the final mix. Indeed, less than half of the tracks have precise intros or endings.

The endless takes led to tempers fraying, with everyone from Ringo to George Martin to chief engineer, Geoff Emerick, and second engineer, Richard Lush, absenting themselves for long stretches to avoid the rows.

Paul went along with many of John's wilder requests, such as recording 'Yer Blues' live in a store-room cupboard, but increasingly he sought to work without him to get peace of mind. In all, a third of the album was completed with only one, two or three group members contributing.

The impact of meditation on *The White Album*

Seeking spirituality and divine powers in the Maharishi's meditation camp in the foothills of the Himalayas between March and April 1968 opened a floodgate of productivity for the Beatles. The empowering effects of meditation, which they practised every day, led to John, Paul and George writing over 20 new songs. Attributed with sparking joy, spontaneity and creativity, meditation led to many of these songs having a light-hearted air. The outdoor gatherings in Rishikesh also encouraged sing-alongs and a string of musical send-ups from ska, Country and Western, boogie-woogie, blues, the Beach Boys, The Who to 30s' dance music.

WHY DON'T WE DO IT IN THE ROAD?
McCartney
Basic track recorded on 9th October 1968 with overdubs on 10th October
Found on *The Beatles* aka The White Album

The sight of two monkeys mating in the road in India amused Paul so much he wrote a song about it. Impressed by the primates' "uncomplicated approach to sex", he brought a similarly brazen style to the recording. Over basic chords with a repetitious lyric he delivers a rough and ever-so-slightly demented vocal. John later said he was hurt at not being asked to play on it, but the track, with its evocation of carnal lust, is perfectly realised in its hokey simplicity between a simple beat and a single guitar. In the previous month, Paul was living the life of a playboy according to several accounts. Separated from long-standing fiancée, Jane Asher, he shared his London house with up to three women.

WILD HONEY PIE

McCartney
Recorded in one take on 20th August 1968
Found on *The Beatles* aka The White Album

It must have been a delight to put this meaningless snippet onto a Beatles' disc, almost as a relief from the weight of expectation their music had received since *Sgt. Pepper's*. A similar piece of light relief, 'Can You Take Me Back?' appears unaccredited between 'Cry Baby Cry' and 'Revolution 9' on *The Beatles*.

WITH THE BEATLES

Recorded in 30 hours. Mixed in 18.45 hours.
Album released 22nd November 1963

Recorded on the run in the middle of a frantic schedule, *With the Beatles* is manically energised with only occasional lapses into exhaustion. Cashing in on their first flush of fame, in the seventy-seven days between the beginning and end of recording* the Beatles played fifty-seven live shows in England, Wales and the Channel Islands, nine radio recordings, four TV shows and five days recording at Abbey Road. So time in the studio had to be disciplined, with songs completed within two hours each. The schedule for 30th July sums this up. Between 10am and 1.30pm 'Please Mr Postman' and 'It Won't Be Long' were made. There was then a journey to central London to record four songs for BBC radio. Returning at 5pm to Abbey Road, 'Till There Was You', 'Roll over Beethoven', a re-make of 'It Won't Be Long' and 'All My Loving' were completed by 11pm. Some of the best performances were captured on this day suggesting the group was rested and prepared. By contrast, on 11-12th September ('Hold Me Tight', 'Little Child', 'I Wanna Be Your Man', 'All I've Got To Do', 'Not A Second Time' and 'Don't Bother Me') their schedule appears to be taking its toll on their sharpness.

The priority given to touring meant songwriting often took place in coaches, vans and hotels. Relentlessly upbeat, this new material reflects the growing hysteria of the crowds that greeted them, but the sombre cover told another story. Shot in half-shadow at the end of a hotel corridor in Bournemouth, the moody photo went against the wishes of their manager, Brian Epstein and EMI, but it signalled a bid for artistic respect and a group with hidden depths.

* 18th July to 12th September 1963

The Beatles discover double-tracking

At first uneasy in the sterile environment of a studio, it began to dawn on the Beatles how they could make larger-than-life renditions of their stage repertoire. Double-tracking vocals, a process that gives a bolder and broader tone became one of their favoured tricks. However, there were drawbacks. For heartfelt or profound lyrics, the double layer of sound can appear artificial. On two-track recording equipment it led to extra tape noise too, blurring the sound quality. They became so enamoured with it that George Martin's efforts to rein them in were over-ruled. The vocals on 'Please Mr Postman' and 'Money' consequently lack the definition of the debut album, while Ringo's poorly-synchronised double-tracking wobbles all over 'I Wanna Be Your Man'. For such reasons John later said he would have loved to have gone back and remixed With the Beatles.

WITHIN YOU WITHOUT YOU
Harrison
John, Paul and George Martin were initially unimpressed with the track according to recording engineer, Geoff Emerick.
"The buzz of buzzes which is the thing that is God, you've got to be straight to get it...be healthy, don't eat meat, keep away from those nightclubs and meditate." Quote from rambling interview George gave to the English hippie newspaper International Times, May 1967.
Basic track recorded 15th March 1967, with overdubs on 22nd March and 3rd April (strings)
Found on *Sgt. Pepper's Lonely Hearts Club Band*

Addressed to a third party, George introduces this as a private conversation of which the listener has no prior knowledge or easy comprehension. Sung in quiet self-contemplation on a single chord, only at two minutes in does he address the listener directly.

Like 'It's Only a Northern Song', its refusal to easily connect with its audience appears to reject John and Paul's sweeter, fantastical vision for *Sgt. Pepper's*, not least for the way its message places spirituality over materialism, a contrast to their unbounded ambition. His words were prescient; by stating the love of a generation was capable of saving the world, he summed up the hopes of idealistic youth from this period.

John and Paul were present for its recording, but respecting George's greater feel for Indian music, they let him work solo. George Martin took a firmer role. Unimpressed, he later called it 'dreary', he added a layer of strings for harmonic interest.

THE WORD
Lennon/McCartney
"Even though I'm not always a loving person, I want to be" John '66
Recorded in the evening of 10th November 1965
Found on *Rubber Soul*

In one of the opening salvos against the US military

involvement in Vietnam, John asks for 'the word' to be given a chance, a message he would later refine as 'Give Peace a Chance'. The horrors of the conflict were starting to be vividly portrayed in the media in 1965, and this vision of global harmony was one of John's earliest responses. He recalled writing it with Paul under the spell of marijuana and as such this is equally about the insights into his own humanity. The lyric tells of how he had been using the splendid isolation afforded by his acquisition of a 15-room home on a private estate to read books on history and religion. This was John in his way getting the university education he never had. Some of this reading featured radical and dangerous ideas. The debunking of New Testament beliefs in Hugh Schonfield's best-selling *The Passover Plot* are directly linked to John's reckless comments in early 1966, that Jesus' disciples were "thick and ordinary" and led him down the path to the reckless statement, "the Beatles are more popular than Jesus Christ".

Ultimately, 'The Word' falls short. Describing its goal as simply 'sunshine' and 'fine' is not persuasive, whilst its dance-beat lacks the impact of the sing-along 'All You Need Is Love' and 'Give Peace a Chance'.

WORDS OF LOVE

Written by Buddy Holly
The 1957 original features one of the first-ever uses of vocal double-tracking
Recorded in three takes on 18th October 1964
Found on *Beatles For Sale*

The demo tapes left behind by Buddy Holly have helped build his legend high. The material he was working on prior to his death at the age of 22, show his talent still evolving and give a tragic sense of a life ended too soon. Honouring this legend the Beatles named themselves along similar lines to Holly's group the Crickets. However, such fan worship meant 'Words Of Love' is simply a tame homage. The arrangement, the unorthodox percussion – Ringo taps a suitcase – are all the same. John and Paul even have identical lead vocals – where normally they would harmonise – to replicate Holly's double-tracked vocals. Also Holly imbued the words with an eroticism beyond their obvious intent – the way 'feel' and 'real' are stretched out is full of insinuation. Notably, where he sings of the words he 'wants' to hear, inadvertently John and Paul sing passively of words they 'long' to hear.

YELLOW SUBMARINE

Music: McCartney   Lyrics: McCartney/Lennon/Donovan Leitch
The singer Donovan gave the line about blue sky and green sea, which echoed a line on the Rolling Stones' 'Paint It Black' which was riding high in the charts.
The basic track was recorded on 26th May 1966 with the group chorus and sound effects added on 1st June
Found on *Revolver*

This mischievous nod to the in-crowd in the guise of a children's song has been so completely co-opted as a wholesome piece of family entertainment that its coded verse has been rendered irrelevant. The double meanings served the purpose of keeping the group amused enough to deliver it with a straight face. The biggest clue to Paul's secret intent is that on John's first LSD trip he hallucinated that he was the captain of a submarine with George and his girlfriend, Patti, as the crew. On record John speaks, in the mannered style of a ship's captain, the words 'full speed ahead'. A yellow capsule-shaped amphetamine was also once apparently nicknamed a 'yellow submarine'. Bob Dylan's ode to drugs, 'Rainy Day Women # 12 and 35' which was then in the charts, has a brass band, a bass drum beat and a sing-along chorus which invites us all to join him in getting 'stoned'. The simple, slow verses were designed to fit Ringo's limited range, while the group chorus absolves him from hitting any high notes. A crowd of friends came to the studio to create a party atmosphere and join in on the chorus. Easy to sing and easy to play, with a three-chord chorus, as many song-writers would attest, this apparent simplicity for such big impact is the product of great skill.

YELLOW SUBMARINE (album)
Album released 13th January 1969, remixed and released again in 1999.

After the disappointment of the lightweight plot for *Help!* the Beatles awaited a cartoon representation of themselves with dread. In an attempt to sabotage the project (which, ironically, they later became rather proud of), they contributed four rushed songs in the summer of 1967 to fulfil their contractual obligation. The worst of these was an early run-through of 'You Know My Name Look up the Number' which the producers United Artists baulked at. 'Hey Bulldog' was recorded in early 1968 and took its place.

YER BLUES
Lennon
"There's a self-conciousness about suddenly singing blues." John 70
The basic track was recorded live on 13th August 1968, with vocal overdubs on 14th August and Ringo's 'two, three, four' count in added on 20th August
Found on *The Beatles* aka The White Album

Unable to sleep properly and in a wretched mood without the comfort of drugs or drink, John found the first weeks of the Maharishi's meditation camp in India especially hard. His mood was not lightened by the presence of his wife, from whom he was becoming increasingly distant. Sardonically, he began to liken his existence to the hopeless figure depicted in Elvis Presley's 'Heartbreak Hotel', a song which re-told the newspaper story of a man who committed suicide in a hotel in Miami. Using the chord structure of 'Heartbreak Hotel' and some of the lyrics, John added sketches on his own wretchedness, the depth of which, he tells us, even made him hate his beloved rock 'n' roll. In this sorry state he dredged up memories of the loss of his mother and father at the age of five. Such disturbing thoughts are matched in the recording made in the claustrophobic setting of the storage room under the stairs at Studio Two at Abbey Road. Notes are missed, timings go astray, the guitars are crudely distorted, the solo is repetitive and the vocals shriek. Similarly, a blunt edit at 3.17 makes no effort to disguise this as a mix of two performances. Playing the blues felt inauthentic to John and the only way he could overcome this was to make it dirty. In this spirit the title became 'Your Blues' instead of 'My Blues' and for good measure, 'Yer Blues'. The contrast with contemporary blues rock bands such as Cream and Fleetwood Mac is stark; whilst they were more interested in musicianship than words, the reverse is true here.

YES IT IS

John Lennon
George struggled here to control a new pedal device that adjusted the tone on his guitar.
The B-side to 'Ticket to Ride'
Recorded in 14 takes on 16th February 1965
Found on *Past Masters*

As an experiment John, Paul and George all sang lead at the same time here. Paul takes the high notes, George is largely in the middle and John is on the lower notes. The effect is hypnotic, removing them of personality, while the dreamy pace and the strangulated cries of a tone-adjusted guitar all accentuate the obsessive nature of the lyric. The third of John's songs to refer to a colour in little over a year the suspicion must be that he was playing some sort of game. Green describes jealousy on 'You Can't Do That', black and blue sum up loss and unhappiness on 'Baby's In Black', but here, the meaning of red, scarlet and blue is enigmatic.

YESTERDAY

McCartney

With 1,600 known recordings, this is the most-covered song of all time. Paul rates Marvin Gaye's 'Yesterday' as his favourite cover version.

The first use of strings on a Beatles' track. George Martin suggested the idea but Paul was resistant and had to be persuaded.

For the 1966 world tour the Beatles performed a version of 'Yesterday' with two guitars, bass and drums.

Paul's vocal and guitar was recorded in two takes on 14th June 1965. The strings were added the same evening.

Found on *Help!*

Composing new tunes became so important for Paul that they started to occur in his dreams. At the height of Beatlemania, the melody for 'Yesterday' arrived while he was in a still semi-conscious state and on opening his eyes he hauled himself over to a piano to figure it out. Incredulous at its long, complex chord cycle, he thought he must have copied it and asked friends to identify the tune. None could. A desire to perfect it led to its being held back further. How long no-one is sure, but it was solely an instrumental from anywhere between six months and a year. The title 'Yesterday' was decided early on but the words only came on 27th May 1965 in a taxi from Lisbon airport to the holiday resort of Albufeira in Portugal. On the 150 mile journey his girlfriend, Jane Asher, fell asleep by Paul's side, which suggests it was the evening and he, too, was tired and in a melancholy mood. Taken at face value he was describing the sudden end of a love affair, but Paul had suffered little heartbreak at this age. Indeed, he sings solemnly, where most cover versions use an anguished tone. An intriguing theory, first put forward in Chris Salewicz's biography *McCartney* (1988) suggests his regret over saying something wrong referred to an outburst on hearing of his mother's death, "What are we going to do without her money?" (both she and her husband brought an income to the McCartney household). The line, which emphasises the suddenness of her death, implies the diagnosis of cancer only two weeks beforehand. Paul has not sought to deny this theory and has admitted he 'may' have been writing about his mother unconsciously.

Another influence was the group's first credible evocation of sadness, 'You've Got to Hide Your Love Away' from February 1965. Here John described his grief as making him feel only two feet tall and in May on 'Yesterday', Paul tells of not being even 'half' of what he was before. In April, on 'Help!' John told of once being happier than 'today', and then Paul followed by singing of being happier 'yesterday'.

Paul wanted to present these thoughts in the bare but powerful style of Bob Dylan, switching from piano, where it had been written, to acoustic guitar, his vocal unadorned with group harmonies. Indeed, Paul harmonised with the guitar so well John was left flummoxed as to how the band could add to it.

While such solo tracks would become increasingly common in the group's career, in 1965 this was a first; it could easily have been billed as by Paul McCartney rather than the Beatles. The addition of strings, an adornment alien to them only emphasised how awkwardly it sat with them. The group being more important than the song, the solution was to bury it as the penultimate track on 'Help!', typically the slot for an album's least-loved track, just before the artless racket of 'Dizzy Miss Lizzy'. It also explains why it was not a single in the UK and why Paul sought to give it away before release. In a decision that blighted their careers, both the rock singer, Chris Farlowe, and Epstein protégé, Billy J Kramer, turned it down as being too sweet, not sensing its inner meaning. However, it has proved, with time, an irresistible cover version for any singer who tackles ballads, some of the most notable versions being by Elvis Presley, Bob Dylan, Ray Charles and Marvin Gaye.

YOU CAN'T DO THAT
Lennon
Offered for the film *A Hard Day's Night* it was rejected by the producers.
Recorded in nine takes on 25th February 1964
Found on *A Hard Day's Night*

The portable jukebox that accompanied John on world tours reveals a playlist dominated by rough, macho tracks at odds with the love songs he wrote with Paul. Their lyrics lay down the law to girlfriends on what is and what is not allowed and warn of the consequences if their rules are ignored. 'Watch Your Step' by Bobby Parker, 'Gonna Send You Back To Georgia' by Timmy Shaw, 'First I Look At The Purse' by The Contours and 'Steppin' Out' by Paul Revere and the Raiders all spoke of male dominance over women. If not quite as nasty, 'You Can't Do That' has a similar message matched with a menacing musical thrust, over which John lets rip with a solo of inspired staccato thrash and stray notes.

Offered for the *A Hard Day's Night* film, it was rejected by United Artists.

YOU KNOW MY NAME (LOOK UP THE NUMBER)

Words: Lennon/McCartney   Music: Lennon/McCartney/Brian Jones
B-side to 'Let It Be'
Basic track recorded 17th May 1967 with overdubs on 7th and 8th June (the latter with saxophone by Brian Jones of The Rolling Stones), the vocals were completed on 30th April 1969
Found on *Past Masters*

When the Beatles heard of Brian Epstein's proposal to sell off part of his management contract in early 1967, they were horrified at the prospect of working with an outsider. In protest, they threatened to record deliberately awful music if the deal went ahead. Months later, after Epstein had relented they remembered this threat when faced with a legal obligation to contribute music to a cartoon over which they had limited creative control. John assumed the task with relish by writing a repetitive eight-word lyric and a risible disjointed arrangement. It was put forward for *Yellow Submarine*, but rejected and stayed in the vaults until 1969 when John returned to it with Paul and added sound effects and voices, though it was another year before it was released. By then the track had become part of John's bid to break what he grandly described as the Beatles myth, by which he meant the perception that somehow everything they did was perfect or magical.

You Like Me Too Much (See It's Only Love page 56)

YOU NEVER GIVE ME YOUR MONEY

Music: McCartney   Words: McCartney/ Lennon
"Me directly lambasting Allen Klein's attitude to us". Paul '98
Largely recorded at Olympic Sound Studios in south-west London, despite appearing on an album named Abbey Road.
Basic track recorded 6th May 1969, with overdubs on 1st, 15th, 30th, 31st

There is a long line of singers who have written bitter lyrics about unfavourable contracts with greedy managers and by these standards Paul's words about Allen Klein are quite tame. Bob Dylan's 'Dear Landlord', The Kinks' 'The Moneygoround' and Queen's 'Death On Two Legs' are all notable in their desperation and rage at their management, while John himself memorably sang that Klein was going to wish he had never been born on 'Steel and Glass', from *Walls and Bridges* in 1974. Paul's restraint was due to Klein not yet having the chance to rip him off, as he rightly feared. Indeed, Klein was in early negotiations to bring the group a better royalty rate for songs such as this, even if 20% went to him. That the others were not listening to these fears put Paul in a lonely position, which is evoked in the way all instruments and vocals are his on the first mournful verse. As if becoming self-conscious of his rift from the group, Paul switches mid-song to an area of his life that was giving him hope. The upbeat section is a satirical ditty composed during an idyllic break (a 'sweet dream') in Linda Eastman's apartment in New York at the end of October 1968, where he first proposed marriage to her. The trip afforded him the chance to explore the edgy streets of the city, unrecognised, unshaven and in a thrift store coat. On a stroll in Harlem he saw a group of children singing in a school playground. This vignette is echoed in the coda, with a nursery rhyme about children going to heaven.

The medley – a mini-opera or just odds and sods?

The B-side to Abbey Road is not the first or the last piece of music to be pieced together, patchwork style, from a series of half-finished songs. John had used four such ideas to create 'Happiness Is a Warm Gun' and The Who did something similar on their mini-opera 'A Quick One While He's Away'. John had witnessed The Who's fiery performance of their song-cycle at The Rolling Stones' Rock 'n' Roll Circus at the tail end of 1968 and he was recorded playing snatches of it weeks later during the Let It Be rehearsals and the Abbey Road medley bears an uncanny resemblance. Pete Townsend's themes are strife, lust, reconciliation, a longing for home and a final redemption ('Her Man's Gone', 'Crying Town', 'Ivor The Engine Driver', 'Soon Be Home' and 'You Are Forgiven'). These are echoed in a similar order here on 'You Never Give Me Your Money', 'Mean Mr Mustard', 'Polythene Pam', 'Golden Slumbers' and 'The End'.

'You Never Give Me Your Money' itself appears to serve as overture for this mini-opera with its tales of business strife, a hard-up student, travel and a children's rhyme about going to heaven.

YOU REALLY GOT A HOLD ON ME

Written by Smokey Robinson
This started a mini-fad for ending songs on a jazz chord (sixths, major sevenths and ninth chords). Five songs on *With The Beatles* use this gimmick (plus 'She Loves You').
Recorded in 11 takes on 18th July 1963
Found on *With The Beatles*

Arguments over the relative merits of Smokey Robinson and the Miracles' 'You Really Got a Hold on me' and this cover version are difficult to settle. The original is slicker, the Beatles' raucous. Ringo's double-tracked cymbals are artless, the Miracles' metronome precise, but the middle section, where the chords clang out and John and George shout 'tighter' (1.40-1.50) is raunchier than what Smokey Robinson envisaged. It also fashions a neat end chord, where the Miracles fade out.

Certainly, the Beatles found it hard to get right – several edits (one can clearly be heard at 0.25) reveal that this is a mix of two takes – but whatever its shortcomings, it would have been a thrill to introduce to the British public. In 1963, Motown records were largely absent from the play-lists of British government-run radio stations due to a mix of limited international promotion and conservative play-lists. Indeed, Motown built up five years of hits in the US before making the UK charts in 1964. This lack of exposure encouraged British bands to claim these hits as their own. The Beatles' covering 'Please Mr Postman' (a US No.1) and 'You Really Got a Hold on Me' and the Rolling Stones recording Marvin Gaye's 'Can I Get A Witness'. Bands sought to stamp ownership by playing a song first and in this way a live version by the Beatles was broadcast on BBC radio on 24th May 1963, a few months after the Miracles' US release.

YOU'LL BE MINE
Lennon/McCartney
Recorded at Paul's home in the spring of 1960.
First released 1995
Found on *Anthology 1*

The flat John and Stuart Sutcliffe shared in Gambier Terrace in the centre of Liverpool whilst art students was so grubby it was the focus of a newspaper scandal story entitled 'Beatnik Horror'. Their carefree existence was typified by the bohemian parties they would attend and John's grotesque drawings which cluttered their rooms. The same dark humour is injected into 'You'll Be Mine' a rough and ready spoof of the quaintly polite 'If I Didn't Care' by The Ink Spots, the 1940s balladeers. There was method in this fooling around. Paul's outrageous falsetto serves as a foil for John's story-telling, a ploy they would use many more times particularly on 'I Want to Hold Your Hand'.

YOU WON'T SEE ME

McCartney
Recorded on 11th November 1965
Found on *Rubber Soul*

The similarity between the melody and rhythm on The Four Tops' 'The Same Old Song' and 'You Won't See Me' is a knowing joke. 'The Same Old Song' was itself a pastiche of The Four Tops' 'I Can't Help Myself' with virtually the same chord progression. The lyrics tell of how the love they sang of in their earlier hit had gone sour and Paul in his way is continuing the joke, by singing of a reversal of the love he had eulogized on 'And I Love Her' and 'Things We Said Today'. The lyrics tell of his temporary split with Jane Asher, who was in Bristol acting in a play and was avoiding his calls. The recording achieves something close to the wall of sound on The Four Tops' releases too, with its use of double-tracked rhythm guitars. The gruelling work needed to finish this and two other songs on the same early hours session is betrayed in John's hoarse backing vocal.

YOUR MOTHER SHOULD KNOW

McCartney
Basic track recorded on 22nd August 1967, with overdubs on 23rd August, 16th and 29th September
Found on *The Magical Mystery Tour*

On first listening this catchy, old-fashioned tune sounds like a break from the craziness of the *Magical Mystery Tour* sessions, but the use of only one verse tells otherwise. In the general 'anything goes' ethos of the project, the first verse is repeated twice, before having one of its lines changed and then repeated twice more. Like much of the *Magical Mystery Tour* the effect is disorientating for a listener, who is never quite sure how far it has progressed. With the pressure of filming their TV special, only a thin recording was made with piano, organ and drums to the fore – unusually for Paul, there is no distinctive bass line.

YOU'RE GOING TO LOSE THAT GIRL
Lennon/McCartney
Recorded in the afternoon of 19th February 1965
Found on *Help!*

The slickest piece of early period Beatles' pop is one of the most overlooked. From its exquisite snare drum roll, to the crisp guitar chord which hangs in the air after the last beat, it has a treasure trove of tricks and harmonies. It is, however, the closest they came to mimicking themselves; its slick repetition of well-worn themes makes it appear a precursor of The Monkees, the studio-created group launched in 1966 to copy them. The sunny, upbeat tune, with its simple tale of relationship advice is a twist on 'She Loves You'. Instead of urging a friend to be closer to his lover, here John warns that he will steal her from him if he is not careful. Betty Everett's 'It's In His Kiss' offers similar advice to a friend and where the backing vocals on Everett's track repeatedly sing 'no' with a wagging finger to her questions, here Paul and George sing 'yes' over and over.

Where's the bass?

'You're Going to Lose That Girl' shows the restrictions placed on the early Beatles' sound with the low presence of bass compared to all other instruments. Their record company, EMI, had strict rules about the how loud bass guitar could be, believing that it would make records jump, causing buyers to return their purchase. In the USA, where vinyl quality was more advanced, this problem had been overcome. Notably, from early 1965, The Byrds' 'Mr Tambourine Man' and The Temptations' 'Get Ready' both featured bass as a dominant instrument.

YOU'VE GOT TO HIDE YOUR LOVE AWAY

Lennon
Features only the second-ever use of a session musician on a Beatles' track – a double-tracked flute solo from Johnny Scott.
Recorded in nine takes on 18th February 1965
Found on *Help!*

A rare audience with John in conversational mode with the listener. For the first time we get the treat of hearing his voice alone, single-tracked, slowly-paced, with every word clearly enunciated. At first languid on the verses, thrillingly it turns loud and abrupt on the chorus. John was baring all to match the style of Bob Dylan with whom he was temporarily infatuated. For this purpose he set the scene of a folky morality tale and yet the words do not reveal a full story, but that he called them 'honest' showed they held some meaning for him, leaving many to wonder what 'love' he was looking to 'hide' away. They make sense of the way the Beatles kept their girlfriends and wives behind the scenes so as to give the impression that they were somehow available to their fans. Most sensationally, the lyrics have been interpreted as being about Brian Epstein's homosexuality. All that is clear is the Bob Dylan stylisation. The first line is near identical to 'I Don't Believe You [She Acts Like We Have Never Met]' from *Another Side of Bob Dylan*. The use of the word 'clowns' can be linked to both 'A Hard Rain's Gonna Fall' and 'Mr Tambourine Man'. The exclamation 'Hey' echoes its use in 'Mr Tambourine Man', an acetate of which was circulating in early 1965. While the use of the folky phrase 'gather around', with its suggestion that the singer is addressing a small group of people in a public setting, is found on 'The Times Are A-Changin' and 'North Country Blues'. John later referred to this era as his 'Dylan days' – on the cover of *Help!* he wears a cap similar to the one worn by Bob Dylan on the cover of *The Times Are A-Changing*. The influence extended to a copy of Dylan's gruff vocal and a purely acoustic accompaniment. John envisioned a harmonica solo, but, realising his homage had gone far enough, a flute solo was used instead, double-tracked with alto and tenor flutes.

BIBLIOGRAPHY

First hand accounts or key data

The Beatles Anthology, Cassell & Co, 2000

The Complete Beatles Chronicle, Mark Lewisohn, Pyramid Books, 1992

The Complete Beatles Recording Sessions, Mark Lewisohn, Hamlyn 1988

Lennon Remembers, Jann S. Wenner, Verso 2000

The Last Interview, David Sheff, Sidgwick and Jackson 2000

Many Years From Now, Paul McCartney edited by Miles, Secker & Warburg 1997

Other works

Apple to the Core: The unmaking of the Beatles, Peter McCabe and Robert D. Schonfield, Brian & O'Keefe, 1972

Be My Baby, Ronnie Spector and Vince Waldron, Harmony Books, 1989

The Beatles, Hunter Davies, revised edition, Arrow Books, 1985

Beatlesongs, William J. Dowlding, Fireside, 1989

Guinness Book of Rock Stars, Dafydd Rees and Luke Crampton, Guinness Publishing 1991

Can't Buy Me Love, Jonathan Gould, Piatkus Books, 2007

Chronicles Volume One, Bob Dylan, Simon and Schuster 2004

Days In the Life, Jonathan Green, Minerva, 1989

Get Back; The Beatles Let It Be Disaster, Doug Sulphy and Ray Schweighardt, Helter Skelter Publishing, 1998

A Hard Day's Write, Steve Turner, Carlton 1994

Here There and Everywhere, Geoff Emerick, Gotham Books 2006

I Me Mine, George Harrison, W.H. Allen 1980

I'll Never Walk Alone, Gerry Marsden and Ray Coleman, Bloomsbury 1993

It Was Twenty Years Ago Today, Derek Taylor, Bantam Press 1987

John, Cynthia Lennon, Hodder Paperbacks 2006

John Lennon In My Life, Pete Shotton and Nicholas Schaffner, Coronet 1983

Let's Go Down The Cavern, Spencer Leigh Vermillion, 1984

Life, Keith Richards, Weidenfeld and Nicolson, 2010

Love Me Do, the Beatles Progress, Michael Braun, Penguin Books, 1964

The Man Who Gave The Beatles Away, Alan Williams and William Marshall, Elm Tree Books 1975

McCartney, Chris Salewicz, St Martins Press, 1986

Mersey Beat: The Beginnings of the Beatles, Bill Harry, Omnibus Press 1977

The Phil Spector Story, Rob Finnis, Rockon 1975

The Quiet One – A Life of George Harrison, Alan Clayson, Sidgwick and Jackson 1990

Revolution in the Head, Ian MacDonald, Pimlico Books, revised edition 2005

Shout! The True Story of the Beatles, Philip Norman, updated edition, Pan Books 2003

Stoned Andrew Loog Oldham, Secker & Warburg, 2000

Summer of Love: The Making of Sgt. Pepper, George Martin, MacMillan 1994

You Never Give Me Your Money, Peter Doggett, Vintage Books 2010

Occasional quotes are taken from interviews or reviews in the New Musical Express, Look, the Daily Mail, the Evening Standard Q and Mojo.